gardening
in the
southwest

BY KATHLEEN NORRIS BRENZEL, PHILIP EDINGER, AND THE EDITORS
OF SUNSET BOOKS

Menlo Park · California

SUNSET BOOKS

Vice President, General Manager: Richard A. Smeby
Vice President, Editorial Director: Bob Doyle
Production Director: Lory Day
Operations Director: Rosann Sutherland
Retail Sales Development Manager: Linda Barker
Executive Editor: Bridget Biscotti Bradley
Art Director: Vasken Guiragossian
Special Sales: Brad Moses

STAFF FOR THIS BOOK

Editor: Kathleen Norris Brenzel
Managing Editors: Zipporah W. Collins, Steven Hiatt
Senior Editor, Sunset Books: Marianne Lipanovich
Senior Writers: Philip Edinger, Jim McCausland
Contributing Writers: Sharon Cohoon, Cathy Crommell

Art Director: Alice Rogers
Photo Editor: Cynthia Del Fava
Assistant Photo Editor: Laura Del Fava
Map Illustrator: Karen Minot
Prepress Coordinator: Eligio Hernandez

Copy Editor: Zipporah W. Collins
Proofreaders: Tom Hassett, Nancy Riddiough
Indexer: Frances Bowles

Cover: Photography by Charles Mann; garden design by
Steve Martino; cover design by Vasken Guiragossian

For additional copies of *Gardening in the Southwest*
or any other Sunset book, call 1-800-526-5111
or visit us at www.sunset.com.

contents

dramatic beauty

The first time I visited the Southwest as a fledgling garden editor for *Sunset* magazine, after a day of poking around home landscapes I jumped into my car and headed north from Phoenix toward Carefree, Arizona. Following my boss's advice to "get to know the desert," I pulled off the road and wandered out across the sandy earth for a closer look at sprays of wildflowers and sculptural cactus, now edged with gold in the twilight. Above me, an endless sky turned pink and pale turquoise as the brilliant orange sun floated toward purple hills. At that moment, I discovered what natives of the region have known all along: that the desert Southwest is vivid, dramatic, and utterly enchanting.

Just as enchanting are the Southwest's home gardens—most in styles unique to the region, with details steeped in a rich cultural heritage: Mexican wood carvings peeking out of flower beds, for instance, or garden furnishings painted in fiesta colors. True, gardening in this rugged landscape offers challenges—aridity, alkaline soils, winds, and summer heat, to name a few. But landscape designers and home gardeners are finding ways to meet these challenges head-on.

This book offers more than gardening tips for the Southwest. It is a collection of ideas that you can borrow or fine-tune as you shape or remodel your own outdoor spaces. Gardens, after all, are not just plants: they are bonus open-air rooms. Whether you tend a tiny Santa Fe courtyard garden or a sprawling tract on the fringes of Phoenix, you can take your design cues from the region's natural landscapes, or its pueblos and haciendas. Or let the colors of a desert sky at sunset inspire your planting palette. Best of all, you can make your garden uniquely yours.

—Kathleen Norris Brenzel
Senior Garden Editor

climate

subtropical to mountain

THE TRULY REMARKABLE THING about the Southwest is that it is so hospitable to plants—the *right* plants, that is. Is anything more splendid than a wild saguaro garden in late winter? When you see a hummingbird suspended in front of an ocotillo flower, or a covey of quail skittering under a palo verde in early evening, would you want to be anywhere else? ◆ Nature has done very well in this sharply defined landscape, ornamenting it with wildflowers in season and a huge array of cacti, trees, shrubs, grasses, and perennials all the time. Few places change more by season—or by elevation. ◆ Gardeners run into trouble only when they try to grow exotic imports that hail from regions cooler, wetter, or less alkaline than here. It's true that you can amend alkaline soil, add shade, and install irrigation—in the right situations, those changes are invaluable. But you can also take the Southwest for what it is: a place whose extremes give it the character we love.

SPANNING PARTS OF THE GREAT BASIN, THE HIGH PLAINS, AND THREE
DESERTS, THE SOUTHWEST IS AN AMERICAN ARCHETYPE.

the southwest difference

The landscape seems bigger than life here, and everything is drawn in sharp relief. Mountain ranges look like cutouts against the evening sky; summer thunderheads rise tens of thousands of feet over a toast-colored landscape; and yuccas, agaves, and cacti flavor the garden with a geometry that isn't available from water-loving exotics.

At lower elevations, gardeners don't even think about winter cold: it's summer heat that sets the horticultural agenda. In the east, on the Llana Estacado, it's wind. And everywhere, aridity affects what you plant and where you plant it.

Yet it isn't the extremes that make Southwest gardens great. It's the ways gardeners temper them: the shade beneath a palo verde, the trickle of a courtyard fountain, the rustle of tall native grasses in a Texas wind, or the flight of *Gaura* flowers on an evening breeze.

Perhaps because mesas, ridges, and rock outcroppings emerge almost everywhere you look (except on the plains), this is the most natural place on earth to bring stone into the garden—or to use the rock that's already there. Gravel makes a moisture-conserving mulch that won't blow away, bigger stones define dry streambeds, and any rock wall ranks with adobe as a just-right foil for Southwest plants.

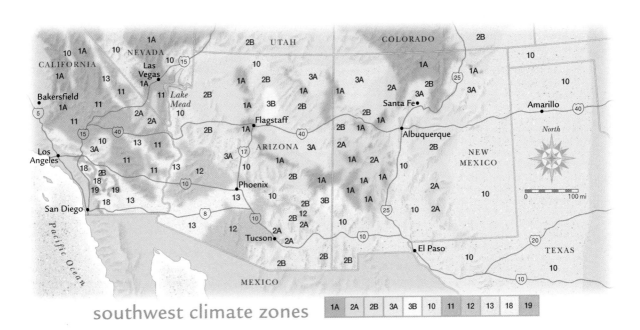

southwest climate zones

| 1A | 2A | 2B | 3A | 3B | 10 | 11 | 12 | 13 | 18 | 19 |

THE LOW DESERTS OF ZONE 13 LIE MOSTLY IN THE COACHELLA, DEATH, AND IMPERIAL VALLEYS AND IN LOWER-ELEVATION PARTS OF THE GILA AND COLORADO RIVER DRAINAGES.

sunset zone 13

The drive along Interstate 10 from Los Angeles to Phoenix gives a good sampling of zone 13. A few miles east of San Gorgonio Pass, the interstate enters the zone as it drops into the Coachella Valley and runs past Palm Springs and Indio. There isn't enough rain for people or agriculture here, but both abound, drinking deeply from canals and aquifers.

From Indio's legendary date palm groves (yes, you can grow dates anywhere in the low desert), the road rises into zone 11 for 25 or 30 miles and then drops back into zone 13 at Desert Center. When you reach Blythe, you're into irrigated agriculture, supplying everything from winter lettuce to early corn and melons. (Watermelons came to the New World with the Spanish and were such an instant hit that their seeds reached native people near the Colorado River delta before the Spaniards got there.)

The first saguaros appear like magic just east of the Colorado River. Their numbers increase as summer precipitation does.

In Phoenix, annual rainfall is only 8 inches, but ubiquitous canals combine with reservoirs on the Gila, Salt, Tonto, and Verde rivers to give city gardeners plenty of water to work with. Artificial waterways have a long history here. Father Eusebio Kino in the 1690s marveled that Casa

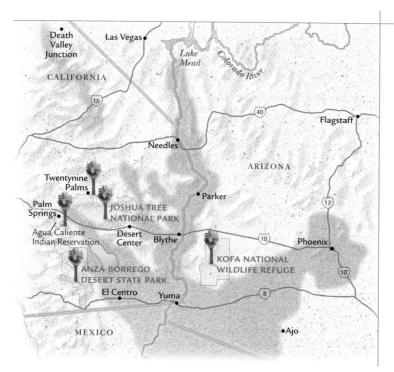

PALM CANYONS California fan palm—the only palm native to the Southwest—grows in canyons all around the low desert. In Arizona, find them at Palm Canyon in Kofa National Wildlife Refuge; in California, at Twentynine Palms Oasis in Joshua Tree National Park; Palm Canyon Oasis on the Agua Caliente Indian Reservation south of Palm Springs; and Borrego Palm Canyon at Anza-Borrego Desert State Park.

Grande "was about a league [three miles] from the river and without water; but afterward we saw that it had a large aqueduct with a very great embankment. . . . This . . . not only conducted the water from the river to the Casa Grande, but at the same time . . . watered and enclosed a champaign [plain] many leagues in length and breadth, and of very level and very rich land."

Native people spent the water on annual food crops and cotton. In today's suburbs, landscape plants have high priority. As pressure on the water supply increases, many gardeners are rethinking that strategy. Native and xeric plants make low-water gardening easy without losing a drop of curb appeal; they're also better-adapted to native soil, whose alkaline pH wreaks havoc with exotics. Water-loving plants can still be worthwhile if used in moderation and for a high payoff. Citrus trees, for example, are beautiful, fruitful, and sweetly fragrant. A modest lawn might be worth its water requirement if you actually spend more time using it than caring for it.

ZONE 13. No part of the Southwest gets hotter—most low desert cities report summer highs averaging 107 to 109°F/42 to 43°C. Phoenix comes in low at 105°F/41°C, while Death Valley pegs the high end with 115°F/46°C. Knowing that annual flowers and vegetables will simply burn out by July, gardeners reverse the planting season: warm-season vegetables go in when the weather starts to cool off in fall, and again when it starts to warm up in late winter. Cool-season plants take center stage from late fall through early spring.

SUMMER AVERAGE HIGH: 105 to 109°F/41 to 43°C

WINTER AVERAGE LOW: 38 to 42°F/3 to 6°C

10-YEAR LOWS: 20 to 27°F/–7 to –3°C

GROWING SEASON: 300 to 365 days

ANNUAL PRECIPITATION: 3 to 8 inches

JOJOBA In 1706, Father Eusebio Kino noted that native people in the Sonoran Desert used the oil of "the important medicinal fruit called jojoba" (*Simmondsia chinensis*) for hair washing, cooking, and treating wounds. Science finally caught up with native wisdom in 1935, when chemists at the University of Arizona in Tucson discovered that the "liquid wax" from jojoba seeds had many of the remarkable characteristics of sperm whale oil.

In the 1930s, the similarity was just an interesting footnote, since whalers supplied all the whale oil anybody wanted. In 1969, things changed when sperm whales were protected under the Endangered Species Conservation Act. Then two years later, the United States forbade the import of sperm whale oil, and the jojoba industry was born.

This Sonoran Desert native plant is now grown commercially in the United States and Mexico, as you'd expect, but also in unexpected places as diverse as Israel, Argentina, and Australia. Jojoba oil is used mostly in cosmetics, but it has great potential for use in industry and cooking as well.

THE INLAND EMPIRE OF CALIFORNIA IS IN ZONES 18 AND 19. PRIMARILY INTERIOR CLIMATE AREAS, THEY FEEL OCEAN INFLUENCE LESS THAN 15 PERCENT OF THE TIME.

sunset zones 18–19

Both zones are associated with mountains: zone 19 often covers low- to mid-elevation slopes, while colder-winter zone 18 extends to the valleys, hilltops, and higher-elevation slopes.

It doesn't take long to fall in love with warm-summer evenings scented with orange blossoms here—California's navel orange industry started in Riverside—and the fragrance of the chaparral after a rain can be intoxicating. But the humidity is generally too low for fuchsias, tuberous begonias, and rhododendrons, so smart gardeners go with the zones' strengths. Mission-style gardens work well here, using such classics as pomegranates, grapes, figs, palms, and olives, plus a more contemporary palette of Mediterranean plants.

Alluvium at the base of the hills and in valley bottoms can be outstanding in both of these zones. Hillside soil is another story: it tends to have little organic matter, fast drainage, and quantities of rock in places. If you want to grow vegetables and flowers that need more moisture-retentive soil, amend with organic matter such as oak-leaf litter, and then top-dress with compost or mulch. Both zones have plenty of summer heat (August days above 90°F/32°C are typical) and a long growing season, so don't be afraid to plant varieties of corn, tomatoes, melons, and peppers that mature late.

Big boulders and river rocks fit perfectly in the hardscape here because they're ubiquitous in the surrounding wildlands. The mountains also become a critical part of design, both as borrowed views and because they create microclimates. A south- or west-facing slope gives you extra sun and heat, and a good reason to plant shade trees. A cooler east- or north-facing slope takes the edge off the heat and offers the chance to plant shade-lovers. If you're gardening in an area that's subject to wildfires, be sure to include a

California missions set the pattern for many of the gardens in zones 18 and 19, combining drought-tolerant Mediterranean flowers, vines, and herbs in low-water landscapes like this one.

buffer of succulents, lawn, or bare earth between your house and adjoining wildlands.

ZONE 18. Zone 18 lies across higher-elevation slopes (temperatures drop 3 to 5°F/2 to 3°C per 1,000 vertical feet), on hilltops whose radiational cooling takes temperatures down on clear winter nights, and in the valleys below, where cold air pools (valley fog is a result). There's enough summer heat to grow desert plants like palo verde, ocotillo, and even saguaro, if you want, and all these do well in the fast-draining mountain soil. But there's also enough cold to grow peonies, *Forsythia*, and a host of deciduous fruit and nut trees.

SUMMER AVERAGE HIGH: 95 to 98°F/33 to 35°C

WINTER AVERAGE LOW: 35 to 39°F/2 to 4°C

10-YEAR LOWS: 17 to 20°F/–8 to –7°C

GROWING SEASON: 228 to 268 days

ANNUAL PRECIPITATION: 11 to 17 inches

ZONE 19. In zone 19 on chilly nights, heavy cold air runs down the slope like water, mixing with warmer air as it drains. That keeps the zone's temperatures a few degrees warmer than in the valleys below and on the hilltops above, both in zone 18. On a zone 19 slope, you can probably succeed with queen palm, Brazilian pepper, amaryllis, 'Haas' avocados, and almonds that wouldn't make it above or below you. You'll also have fewer problems with citrus here, since January nights usually average around 40°F/4°C.

SUMMER AVERAGE HIGH: 90 to 97°F/33 to 36°C

WINTER AVERAGE LOW: 39 to 42°F/4 to 6°C

10-YEAR LOWS: 22 to 28°F/–6 to –2°C

GROWING SEASON: 285 to 345 days

ANNUAL PRECIPITATION: 10 to 17 inches

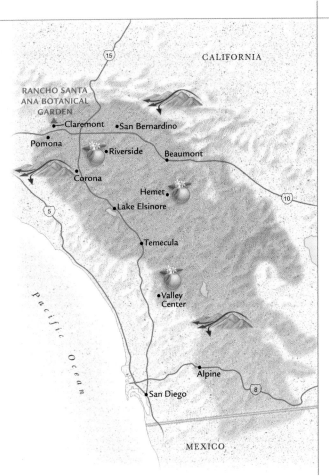

SANTA ANA WINDS Ferocious dry winds roar out of the desert and across Southern California every fall and winter, raising temperatures, drying out plants, and whipping up fires. They come through the passes between the desert and the coast, but they're named for Santa Ana Canyon, one of the first places early settlers noticed them.

ORANGE GROVES In 1875, Eliza Tibbets planted California's first navel oranges, spawning a citrus revolution in the state. You can see one of the original two trees, which still bears fruit, on Magnolia Avenue at Arlington Avenue in Riverside. Hemet is a center for grapefruit.

INCLUDING HIGH ELEVATIONS OF FOUR DESERTS IN SIX STATES, ZONE 10 COVERS MORE TERRITORY FROM EAST TO WEST THAN ANY OTHER SOUTHWESTERN CLIMATE ZONE.

sunset zone 10

Most of zone 10 lies between 3,000 and 5,000 feet, so snow is an occasional visitor, especially in the east. The principal challenges here are aridity, alkaline soil, periodic drought, and persistent wind, but they're balanced by plenty of sunshine and a long growing season.

More rainfall and less heat distinguish most of zone 10 from zone 11. Precipitation is the big variable in this zone. It increases from west to east, with the bulk coming in winter in the west and in summer in the east. Just consider July-through-September rainfall totals across the zone: in Mojave, summer rain accounts for about 10 percent of the annual total; in Phoenix, 33 percent; in Las Cruces, 52 percent. Cities along the Mexican border get more summer rain, in fact, than Seattle does.

Wind is a factor throughout zone 10, especially when it comes in spring, just as seedlings and landscape plants are sending out tender new leaves. The best long-term solutions are to plant big-leafed plants in sheltered places, plant a windbreak, and water in the evening after the wind has died down. Also make the most of ornamental grasses: they're designed for wind, which pollinates them, disperses their seed, animates them, and makes gentle music in their leaves.

ZONE 10. Though the growing season is long here, gardens experience sharp winters, with most places getting 75 to 100 nights below 32°F/0°C. That favors deciduous fruits, though late frosts can work against apricots and almonds. Expect 6 to 8 months between freezes—plenty of time to ripen late-maturing fruits and vegetables, if you can protect them from the wind. Annual rainfall rises from about 4 inches in the Mojave Desert to 19 inches in the high plains of Texas. Summer high temperatures, which run about 95°F/35°C in most of the zone, and above 100°F/38°C in California and Nevada, make shade trees very important.

SUMMER AVERAGE HIGH: 92 to 102°F/33 to 39°C

WINTER AVERAGE LOW: 22 to 32°F/–6 to 0°C

10-YEAR LOWS: –10 to 10°F/–23 to –12°C

GROWING SEASON: 190 to 250 days

ANNUAL PRECIPITATION: 4 to 19 inches

facing page Thunderheads billow above the deserts on late summer afternoons, often delivering quick, heavy cloudbursts. above The color and flavor of fire, chiles ripen easily in zone 10's warm summers.

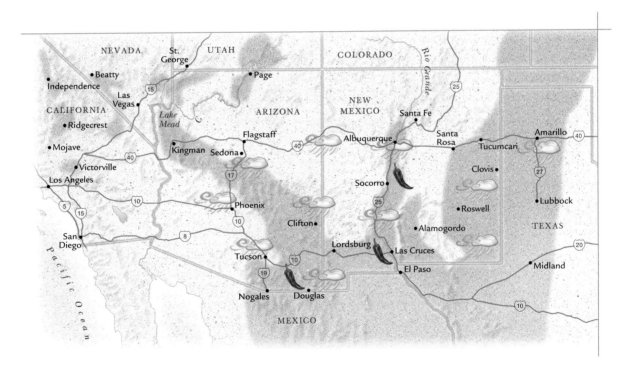

CHILE COUNTRY Long hot summer days in this zone are perfect for growing chile peppers. Commercial growers are located here; they focus on relatively mild varieties of New Mexico pod-type peppers. Home gardeners in the state's northern regions grow varieties that turn red earlier and are generally hotter.

MONSOONS Mexican monsoons surge north into Arizona and New Mexico from July through September. Joined by lookalike storms that originate farther north, they can supply half this zone's annual rainfall.

THE INTERMEDIATE TO HIGH DESERTS OF CALIFORNIA AND NEVADA, FROM LAS VEGAS TO ANTELOPE VALLEY, ARE IN ZONE 11. MOST OF THE ZONE FALLS IN THE 2,000- TO 3,000-FOOT ELEVATION RANGE.

sunset zone 11

Zone 11 is Joshua tree country and includes some of the best wild-flower displays anywhere. But, with as little as 4 inches of rainfall annually, the climate demands water conservation. Gardeners in Las Vegas are doing better than most at shifting from water-intensive to low-water gardens. The switch was driven in part by a Las Vegas Valley population that has quintupled in 20 years, nearly maxing out the area's Colorado River water allotment, and in part by skyrocketing water rates. To demonstrate the possibilities of low-water gardening, the Las Vegas Valley Water District developed the Gardens at the Springs Preserve (see Resources, page 189). It also offers plant lists to help home gardeners grow low-water gardens. Gardeners who convert conventional gardens to low-water ones can get a cash rebate per square foot from the Southern Nevada Water Authority.

California poppy carpets the ground under a cholla in early spring. In the desert, this much-loved state flower is an ephemeral, racing from seed to blossom in just a few weeks. Extent of bloom depends on rainfall: in a good year, poppies can paint whole hillsides orange and yellow.

Shade has high value in zone 11 gardens, and lots of great trees beyond olives and date palms can do the job. Try desert willow for flowers, Chinese pistache for fall color, escarpment live oak for evergreen leaves, and Italian stone pine for statuesque beauty. 'Phoenix' mesquite is a good shade producer, as are many of the palo verdes.

ZONE 11. This medium to high desert zone is warmer all year than higher-elevation zones 1–3 and 10 and has a longer growing season. It also has less rain and more wind than adjacent parts of zone 10. Day–night temperature swings are wide, with mild nights following 100°F/38°C August days, and 60°F/16°C days following frosty January nights. Wind and low rainfall make gardening a challenge here, especially in California's Antelope Valley. In Las Vegas, some summer rain helps matters, but supplemental water is essential, and windbreaks are very useful.

SUMMER AVERAGE HIGH:
93 to 105°F/34 to 41°C

WINTER AVERAGE LOW:
31 to 38°F/−1 to 3°C

10-YEAR LOWS:
10 to 17°F/−12 to −8°C

GROWING SEASON:
216 to 267 days

ANNUAL PRECIPITATION:
4 to 11 inches

JOSHUA TREES If you asked Dr. Seuss to design a signature plant for this zone, it couldn't look more improbable than the Joshua tree (*Yucca brevifolia*). See the best of these trees at Joshua Tree National Park, www.nps.gov/jotr, (760) 367-5500.

POPPIES California wildflowers rank among the world's most spectacular. See them at Antelope Valley California Poppy Reserve (www.calparksmojave.com). Sown in drifts, the flowers—mostly poppies, goldfields, lupine, cream cups, and coreopsis—can give your garden pyrotechnics, too. Water extends their bloom.

HIGH-STAKES HORTICULTURE Drive through Las Vegas to feast your eyes on queen palms, California pepper trees, bougainvilleas, cannas, and citrus. All are good bets—until the inevitable hard freeze wipes them out. Try the MGM/Mirage Hotel for a sure winner: a spectacular domed tropical rain forest filled with palms, bromeliads, and orchids.

ARIZONA'S INTERMEDIATE-ELEVATION DESERT, LYING IN ZONE 12, IS ONE OF TWO PLACES IN THE INTERIOR WHERE MEANINGFUL YEAR-ROUND GARDENING IS POSSIBLE. ZONE 13 IS THE OTHER.

sunset zone 12

Like zone 13, zone 12 enjoys a climate in which most annuals and vegetables can be planted in fall, after the heat is past, or in spring, before the big heat comes. There's enough cold to set fruit on apples and pears, yet the climate is mild enough for citrus trees (they'll suffer frost damage in freezes every 10 years or so and in cold microclimates).

Temperatures push above 90°F/32°C in May and top out above 100°F/38°C in July. Then Arizona's legendary whipped-cream thunderheads move in, shading the landscape, raising the humidity, and dousing the land with life-giving cloudbursts. The temperature starts to fall, and both plants and people revive.

In nature, zone 12 has some of the most lush desert gardens in North America—a fact not lost on home gardeners, who soon learn how slowly many cacti grow (a half inch per year is common). Desert perennials, trees, and annuals are better bets for giving quick shape, fill, and volume to the garden. And nothing says "oasis" better than palms, of which at least ten kinds grow well here.

More conventional garden plants also succeed if you use water carefully. Start with a good drip-irrigation system, and mulch well to get the most out of your water supply. Or put a few thirsty plants in big containers, where you can hand-water them. Angel's trumpet, for example, can make a huge impact in a half wine barrel.

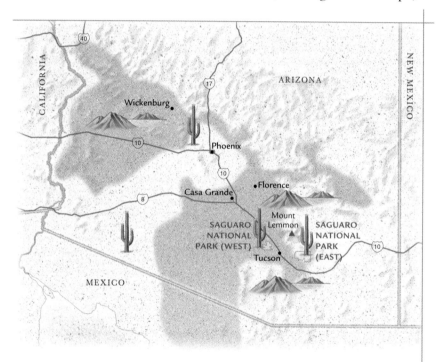

SAGUARO COUNTRY Foresting the most botanically rich desert in North America (the Sonora), saguaros thrive where winters are mild and hot summers are tempered by monsoons. Visit them at Saguaro National Monument, www.nps.gov/sagu, (520) 733-5100. You can grow them, but the arms don't appear for 50 years.

SKY ISLANDS Sky islands that rise out of the zone 12 desert show how topography tempers climate. Rain increases with elevation, temperatures drop 3 to 5°F/2 to 3°C per thousand feet, and forest plants enter the mix. On Mount Lemmon near Tucson, look for Douglas fir, ponderosa pine, and aspen; they grow at much lower elevations in the northern parts of the state.

ZONE 12. Warmer in winter than zone 10, but not as warm as zone 13, this is a cool-winter, hot-summer climate, with a long growing season (although not as long as zone 13's). Summer monsoons provide about half the year's precipitation from Tucson to the Mexican border. Moving north, summer rainfall drops off; Wickenburg, for example, gets just 38 percent of its rain in summer.

SUMMER AVERAGE HIGH: 100 to 107°F/38 to 42°C

WINTER AVERAGE LOW: 31 to 37°F/–1 to 3°C

10-YEAR LOWS: 17 to 20°F/–8 to –7°C

GROWING SEASON: 230 to 270 days

ANNUAL PRECIPITATION: 8 to 11 inches

Nothing says "Sonoran Desert" like a forest of saguaro cactus. With arms stretched out toward the light and the rain, these cacti bear their edible fruits in early summer. When the monsoons arrive, the 50-foot giants expand to hold the extra water.

THE 5,000- TO 7,000-FOOT MOUNTAIN REGIONS OF ARIZONA AND NEW MEXICO
FALL IN ZONES 1–3, TYPICALLY WITH MILD SUMMERS AND SNOWY WINTERS.

sunset zones 1–3

The warm but not scorching summers of zones 1–3 give perennial and annual flowers longer bloom seasons than these plants have in zones 10–12 at lower elevations. When snow comes early and stays, it provides an insulating blanket that protects plants from the hard freezes that may follow. If the winter is dry, or if a garden is on a south-facing slope where snow doesn't remain for long, the plants are more susceptible to frost damage.

As you drive up into zones 1–3 from lower elevations, you can see the climate transitions in the plant communities. One-seed junipers gradually give way to piñon pines, then Rocky Mountain junipers come into the mix, and up higher Gambell oaks appear. Ponderosa pine forests take over at even higher elevations, sometimes mixing with fir and spruce, depending on where you are in the zones.

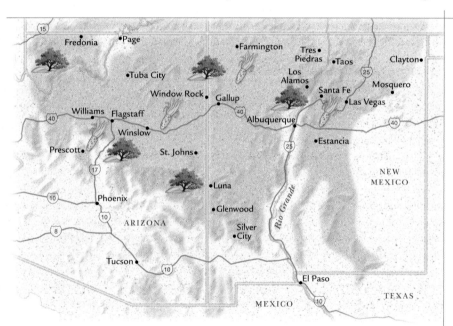

Gardeners here can make the most of the mountains' numerous microclimates. South and west slopes are the hottest and brightest, so they usually benefit from shade trees and require tough varieties of annuals and perennials that won't burn out. North and east slopes are better suited for big-leafed plants and species that do well in partial shade.

Mountain soils are usually low in organic matter and fast-draining. Amend flower and vegetable beds with compost or rotted manure before planting, and mulch everything to hold in the moisture and gradually improve the soil beneath.

HOPI SWEET CORN Short growing season, wind, and drought make standard corn nearly impossible to raise here. But Hopi sweet corn is one local variety that does grow well. Local Hopi Indians selected it over a long period of time as much for the challenging regional conditions as for the corn's flavor.

PINE FORESTS Piñons—classic cool-zone pines—are much loved around Santa Fe for their dense foliage and the edible seeds in their cones. The trees need water to thrive. During long, wet periods, the forests spread downslope; during dry cycles, they recede. If you have piñon pines on your property, you may be able to save them from drought stress by giving them a deep soaking each month.

Tinted yellow and russet-orange by cool October nights, autumn leaves mark the clear transition from summer to winter in high-elevation zones 1–3. This is where deciduous plants are most effective in the Southwest and where seasons are most sharply defined.

ZONES 1–3. Because these zones are located at relatively high elevation, they're the Southwest's coldest zones in winter and mildest interior zones in summer. The frost-free growing season averages 4 to 5 months, so it makes sense to start flowers and vegetables from seedlings and use floating row covers to protect against frost both early and late in the season. Rainfall is highest in the southern parts of these zones (where summer monsoons are a factor), the eastern parts (where squall-line showers bring moisture in spring), and the higher elevations.

SUMMER AVERAGE HIGH:
    78 to 93°F/26 to 34°C

WINTER AVERAGE LOW:
    5 to 22°F/–15 to –6°C

10-YEAR LOWS:
    –10 to –30°F/–23 to –34°C

GROWING SEASON:
    90 to 160 days

ANNUAL PRECIPITATION:
    9 to 21 inches

IN ONE GARDEN, ANGEL'S TRUMPET COMES BACK YEAR AFTER YEAR; IN ANOTHER
NEARBY, IT FREEZES AND DIES. WHY? MICROCLIMATES MAY BE AT WORK.

microclimates

Every house—and the lot it sits on—sets up its own pattern of microclimates—spots seasonally warmer, colder, or windier than their surrounding areas. The home's four exposures differ in how much heat each receives from the sun; this, in turn, depends on latitude. In Tucson, for example, south and west walls receive much more heat than north and east walls.

Microclimates can cause problems, or they can work to your advantage. The same dappled shade that reduces the number of flowers on a rose can keep a potted gardenia from scorching. Look around your property, and identify your microclimates. Then match them with the appropriate plants; modify microclimates where you can, by planting hedges for windbreaks or trees for shade.

❧ SOUTH AND WEST WALLS concentrate heat by reflecting sunlight. Masonry walls also soak up sun and radiate it back to plants at night. The greater the mass of the wall, the more heat the adobe, brick, or stone will hold. In mild-summer climates, the extra heat can help you ripen tomatoes, but in hot-summer climates, you need to screen such walls with trees or vines to shade and cool them.

❧ NORTH WALLS are nearly always shaded and lend themselves to leafy gardens of shade-loving plants. They can define the coolest spot on the property in hot-summer climates.

❧ EAST WALLS bask in morning sun but are sheltered from the scorching afternoon sun: perfect for perennials that need plenty of light to set flowers but can't handle much heat.

❧ SHADE TREES, ramadas, and arbors create understory environments that are cooler in the day and warmer at night and in winter than open ground. That temperature difference can keep borderline plants from burning in summer or freezing in winter.

❧ EAVES provide some shade for plantings beneath them and confer a little extra frost (or hail) protection to tender plants in cold-winter areas. But they also block rain, so you must remember to water under eaves; soaker hoses make it easy.

❧ WIND desiccates plants, stunts growth, breaks branches, and shreds leaves. A hedge or shelter belt (row of trees) breaks the force of wind better than a wall, protecting the area on its leeward side for 10 to 20 times its height.

❧ BREEZEWAYS can concentrate wind, increasing its speed, so that it shreds big-leafed plants. Buffer the upwind side with a windbreak, or line the passage with wind-resistant plants such as conifers and tall grasses.

❧ COOL AIR pools in low places. It can also dam up behind hedges and houses that run across slopes. In mild-winter climates, fruit trees like apples, cherries, peaches, pears, and apricots can use the extra chill to set fruit. But choose warmer-winter spots for subtropicals.

❧ SLOPING GROUND drains cold air downhill just like water. As the air moves, it mixes and becomes warmer than the air on hilltops above and in valleys below. That's why oranges often grow best on sloping ground from Riverside to Tucson.

WET YEARS, DRY YEARS
Much of the Southwest gets half its precipitation in winter and half in summer. If either half fails, or if both halves are diminished, there's drought.

Summer rainfall comes largely from monsoons, and is most pronounced from Tucson to Las Cruces. Monsoons originate in the Gulf of Mexico: easterly trade winds pick up moisture and carry it to northwestern Mexico, where it either falls as rain or picks up more moisture from the Gulf of California. As the interior of our Southwest warms up, rising hot air creates a vacuum that pulls Mexican monsoons north.

Monsoons usually produce cloudbursts that can soak one piece of ground and leave the next hill dry. Smart gardeners catch roof runoff in cisterns or clean garbage cans. They direct pavement and garden runoff into low swales, where it can soak into the ground and water their plants. Monsoons are heaviest along the border, where they account for about half the annual rainfall; they diminish as they move north. Along the Utah-Colorado border, they combine with rain generated by westerlies to produce about a third of that region's annual rainfall.

Winter rainfall in the Southwest comes from Pacific storms. In the California deserts, it accounts for about 80 percent of the 5-inch annual rainfall. In Arizona and New Mexico, winter rains bring 50 to 70 percent of annual rainfall—more at higher elevations and farther north.

EL NIÑO—warmer-than-normal sea surface temperatures in the central and eastern equatorial Pacific—usually directs the subtropical jet stream, and with it the winter storm track, right over the Southwest, tending to bring wet winters.

LA NIÑA—cooler sea surface temperatures, the opposite of El Niño's—usually directs the subtropical jet stream much farther north, giving the Southwest dry winters.

For pragmatic gardeners, it's enough to know that drought can develop anytime. If you plant and irrigate keeping water conservation in mind, you won't have to change your habits much when the inevitable dry years come, to keep your plants going—and you'll still have a beautiful garden when the wet years return.

El Niño conditions

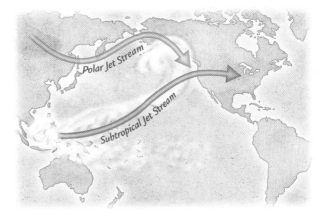

La Niña conditions

ARID PLACES LIKE THE SOUTHWEST USUALLY HAVE HIGHLY ALKALINE AND SALTY SOILS WITH LOW ORGANIC CONTENT, BUT GARDENERS CAN MEET THE CHALLENGE.

matching plants and soils

The Southwest has plenty of good earth, as native farmers have been proving for millennia. But it also has its share of marginal soils. To create the best garden, you can alter your soil to match your plants or choose plants that grow well in the soil you have.

In most gardens, it makes sense to do a little of both. Devote a modest area to your passion: a rose garden, say, or a vegetable plot. Amend the soil, and make it perfect. But use the lion's share of your landscape for drought-tolerant natives and low-water exotics. The range has grown explosively in the past 20 years. Plant collectors and breeders offer a rich palette of such groups as *Acacia*, *Agastache*, *Agave*, *Calliandra*, *Cassia*, grasses, mesquite, palms, *Penstemon*, and *Salvia*. You save soil preparation in the short run and water in the long run—and have a fabulous landscape.

If nothing seems to grow well in your garden, test your soil for imbalances that can harm even native plants. Consult your Cooperative Extension Office.

◈ SOIL pH measures acidity and alkalinity. Most plants do best in soil whose pH is around 7 (neutral), though many plants can tolerate a pH as low as 5.5 (acid) or as high as 8 (alkaline, or basic). Arid parts of the Southwest usually have alkaline soils. When the pH exceeds 8, essential micronutrients such as iron become unavailable to plants.

◈ SALINITY builds up in soil that doesn't get enough water. A reading of 4 millimhos per cubic centimeter is safe, while anything above 12 usually burns leaves and prevents roots from taking up water. To cut salinity in half, flush your soil with 1 foot of water; repeat to halve it again.

◈ NUTRIENTS feed plants. If your soil is low in some of them, add more. If any is high enough to be toxic—as boron can be—leach it out of the soil with deep irrigations.

◈ DRAINAGE lets roots breathe and lets water percolate down, carrying salt out of the root zone. To test your drainage, dig a planting hole, and fill it with water. After it has drained, fill it again: it should then lose at least 4 inches of water in 4 hours. Hardpan, caliche (discussed next), and heavy clay all impede drainage. You can sometimes break a "chimney" through hardpan or caliche to porous soil below. If clay is the problem, amend it with organic matter.

◈ CALICHE is soil that's cemented together with calcium carbonate (limestone); it occurs on the surface or beneath topsoil and may be gravel-like pebbles or a solid layer like concrete, from several inches to several feet thick. Neither water nor roots can easily penetrate it. When it's not far below the surface, salt builds up in the soil above it. If you find caliche when you dig a hole, either break through it with a jackhammer or build a mound or raised bed over it.

◈ TEXTURE describes the amount of sand, silt, and clay in soil. Perfect soil is a balanced mix of all three. Soil with too much sand won't hold nutrients or water. Soil with too much clay won't drain water or hold enough air. Most texture problems can be corrected by digging in a 3- to 4-inch layer of organic matter, such as compost, peat, or rotted manure.

GROWING EDIBLES

Author Gary Paul Nabhan is passionately interested in the botany, ecology, cultures, geography, and history of the Southwest. He's the cofounder of Native Seeds/SEARCH, recipient of a MacArthur Fellowship, director of the Center for Sustainable Environments at Northern Arizona University, inveterate home gardener, and member of various boards connected with nature, from the national parks to Amazonia. Here are some of his thoughts on food gardening in the Southwest.

◈ ON PLANTING: First, talk to elders who have been growing edibles in the Southwest for a long time. They know when to sow seed, how to amend soil; they understand companion planting and spacing. When I moved here, I talked with Hopi and Navajo people about growing corn. They plant 12 seeds in a hill instead of in rows. The roots then intertwine so the spring winds won't dislodge them. Groups of corn also get better pollination than rows do.

◈ ON SUSTAINABLE GARDENING: Sustainability starts with water and energy use. If we keep using water at the rate we are now, for example, Lake Powell will be dry by 2027. With the right plants, we can use less. We have to choose crops to fit the environment rather than trying to remake the environment to fit the crops. And we have to garden in ways that replenish the soil, not deplete it.

◈ ON SEED: Regionally adapted seed is especially important in the desert because our growing conditions are so different from those elsewhere. I grow Hopi sweet corn, which is perfectly adapted where I live [near Flagstaff]; it ripens in a short season and outproduces other corn here. The Hopi got their seed at a world's fair in the 1890s; then they selected the best plants for replanting year after year. You can buy seed at Native Seeds/SEARCH; but after that, select your seed from what you grow. Gradually you'll develop a strain that's best adapted in your own garden. All of us can be plant breeders.

◈ ON SOIL IMPROVEMENT: Desert soil is low in organic matter, high in pH. The best way to improve it is with leaf mulch from native trees like mesquite, catclaw acacia, ironwood, and palo verde. These are all legumes, and the duff beneath them contains microbes that help plants. Wild tepary beans grow under mesquite trees in part because the duff may contain a growth-fostering inoculum.

◈ ON WATER: All my buildings have rain barrels, and any rainfall I can't capture is channeled into a series of basins in my fields. When the soil is saturated, the runoff goes into a sunken pond lined with bentonite. I retrieve it with buckets or, when I need a lot at once, with a submersible pump powered by a solar panel. I also mulch my plants with a 2- to 3-inch layer of rock from volcanic cinders. It holds in moisture and keeps the soil underneath cool, like straw mulch, but with fewer bug problems.

◈ ON REASONS TO GROW FOOD HERE: It's more efficient to grow food in the desert than to import it. This place has an ancient history of agriculture; why would we think we can't grow our own food here? It's possible to get phenomenal yields.

SOUTHWEST STYLE

cultural
influences

SOUTHWEST GARDENERS DRAW ON A RICH CULTURAL HERITAGE FROM NATIVE AMERICANS, MEXICAN SETTLERS, AND SPANISH MISSIONARIES IN THE PLANTS AND TECHNIQUES THEY USE.

For at least 2,000 years, southwestern native people have farmed the desert landscape. Hohokam, Mogollon, and Anasazi people irrigated the landscape to raise calabashes, corn, beans, cotton, and squash; peppers grew wild. Today's Pueblos raise most of the same crops. Add potatoes and tomatoes (also American natives), and you have the pillars of contemporary vegetable gardens everywhere.

Early on, influences from Spain and Mexico were also felt in the Southwest. Just after 1700, Father Eusebio Kino described plants already grown in the region. In addition to vineyards and sugarcane, he wrote, "there are many Castilian fruit trees, such as fig-trees, quinces, oranges, pomegranates, peaches, apricots, pear-trees, apples,

mulberries, pecans, prickly pears, etc., with all sorts of garden stuff, such as cabbages, melons, watermelons, white cabbage, lettuce, onions, leeks, garlic, anise, pepper, mustard, mint, Castilian roses, white lilies." The descendants of those plants are here today.

Plants spread with religion: the church allowed Catholic priests to build missions only in places that could be agriculturally self-sufficient. Father Kino turned his attention to the Southwest only after he failed to find an acceptable combination of water and fertile land in Baja California. When he ventured into the area that is now Arizona and New Mexico, he brought wheat, improved varieties of vegetables from Mexico, and farming techniques that turned each mission into a plant-introduction station.

Meanwhile, botanists working in Mexico collected zinnias, dahlias, and marigolds that proved their worth as ornamentals in the Southwest. Locals were wowed by the beauty at their feet in the surrounding hills and deserts. Making informal collections, they brought in everything from blanket flower to Apache plume, cactus to dalea.

The walled-garden style of the Spaniards, with its Moorish roots, actually fit well with the Pueblo style of enclosed spaces, terraces, and adobe walls. The two blended seamlessly, and some of the Southwest's most beguiling gardens today take their design cues from these early styles. Adobe walls cast shade, break up the wind, and provide the perfect backdrop for southwestern plants.

Technology, unfortunately, worked against this strong, simple fusion of styles. In the 20th century, as a growing system of dams, canals, pumps, and pipes made water cheap and easy to get, many gardeners imported the lawns, trees, and shrubs that look natural in the wetter places they came from but distinctly out of place here.

Change has come slowly, urged along by one of the Southwest's 50-year droughts. In early 2004, the Albuquerque City Council reversed neighborhood covenants that mandated lawns where water-thrifty plants make infinitely more sense. And a growing band of dedicated nursery people are offering ever more drought-tolerant plants to Southwest gardeners. Many of the plants are native, but many more are native to dry-summer climates from around the world. These are the right plants in the right place, and nothing could be better.

facing page A masonry court-yard that shelters plants from wind has an overhead arbor to make shade and support vines. top Peppers are traditionally dried and stored on *ristras*—strings—that usually hang from the poles used to build adobe houses; in a pinch, even an old truck will do. above A prickly pear grows up in a field of purple desert wildflowers. It's just as stunning in the garden as in the wild.

gardens

SOUTHWEST STYLE·DESERT EDGE
COURTYARDS·WATERWISE·NATIVE
SCULPTURAL·SAGUARO COUNTRY
FANTASY·SMALL·RETREATS
NATURALISTIC·WILDLIFE
ENTERTAINING·FAMILY
HIGHER-ELEVATION·WINTER

inspiring ideas

THERE'S NO MISTAKING a true Southwest garden: its style is born of a dramatic natural landscape of deserts and mountains, a climate of hot sun and summer rains, and a mix of cultures rooted in pre-European America, Mexico, and Spain. ◆ Garden walls may be angular or softly sculpted, painted in muted earth tones, soft pastels, or bright jewel colors. Plants are often bold and dramatic—curvy saguaros, bony ocotillos, or gnarly piñon pines rise among softening sprays of wildflowers or wispy grasses. Most likely, there's a ramada or other shade structure for shelter from hot sun, a patio or courtyard with a trickling fountain, and a *chimenea* or fireplace for warmth on chilly evenings. ◆ But it's the individual touches, the furnishings and accessories, that give the Southwest landscape its character. That's true whether you garden on a sprawling tract of land abutting the natural desert or in a small urban courtyard.

left Indigenous pueblo architecture inspired the massive walls and angular planes, but this home design is distinctly modern. Plants surrounding the spa were selected for heat tolerance as well as color.

right Thick walls, arched openings, and intricate wrought iron-work are legacies of Latin America's Spanish-colonial period in this Las Vegas home. Even the cauldron pot, holding a young palm and overflowing with ivy geranium, is a clear nod to Mexican influence.

right In a previous life, this pedestal creation might have been a fountain, birdbath, or baptismal font—but now it gets new purpose as garden sculpture. Low-growing greenery fills its interior without detracting from the vessel.

below The wooden gate is characteristic of Southwest gardens. Here it is weathered and topped with turned staves that allow a glimpse of the interior. A geranium splashes over the top of the walls.

below Throw pillows in traditional Navajo blanket patterns use natural dyes for a range of earthy tones and aniline dyes to add a range of brilliant colors to the palette.

above Suspended from roof beams, a *ristra* of drying chiles makes the quintessential Southwest statement—a regional tradition that reaches back to pre-Columbian times.

above What could have been a blank wall pierced by a plain doorway is now a visual focal point painted in folk-art style. The depiction of a Southwest Mexican cathedral uses exaggerated perspective and abundant sky to create the illusion of depth on a flat surface.

right A lavish planting highlights drought-tolerant aloes, organpipe and barrel cacti, and agaves. The simple wood-plank bench and natural stone pavers accent the dramatic sculptural forms of the featured plants.

A GARDEN ON THE EDGE OF PRISTINE DESERT IS AT ITS BEST WHEN IT MAKES A SUCCESSFUL TRANSITION FROM AN ARTFUL DESIGN TO THE NATURAL LANDSCAPE.

desert edge gardens

The desert edge garden subtly blends the two areas, blurring the boundaries between cultivated garden and the desert beyond. To intersect with the wild, you can angle a patio to face a vista, use low walls instead of tall ones to underline— not block—a view, or put windows in tall walls to frame the wild landscapes. You can install little ponds on your garden's boundaries to entice wildlife onto your property or add steps leading up or down into the desert.

Drifts of golden-flowered brittlebush that meander in graceful swaths right up to your front door can give the impression that they simply ignored the garden's boundaries and invited themselves in from the wild. An infinity-edge swimming pool facing the desert frames distant views while reflecting sky and clouds.

The most effective desert edge gardens repeat elements that are found in the surrounding natural landscape—the trees and rocky outcrops, the shapes and scents of foliage and blossoms, the colors of sand and stone.

above Just two steps up from ground level, this flagstone patio is sited to capture the maximum panoramic view of rugged mountains at the valley's margin. A low wall and middle-height plants largely screen out nearby homes between the mountains and the patio.

right Perched high on a hillside, an observation-deck patio affords a sweeping vista of the valley and the distant mountains framing it. Floor-to-ceiling windows and glass doors invite the view indoors, too.

facing page On a clear day you can see forever. The glassy water of this free-form infinity-edge pool makes a striking transition from stone-covered patio to the Sonoran Desert beyond. Water flows over the pool's rim into a downhill basin from which it recirculates.

above Although contemporary in design, this house, patio, and pool are completely at home in the natural desert landscape. Tucked into the patio, an infinity edge pool is a serene oasis edging Scottsdale's desert. An ironweed tree next to the wing wall makes a striking silhouette against the evening sky.

right Water for the pool shown above cascades through a canterra-stone scupper in the side of a raised stone platform at one end of the pool. A solitary potted century plant (*Agave americana*) is a piece of living sculpture.

facing page Rugged native boulders frame an artfully designed naturalistic pool. Water enters via a small waterfall over the boulders, then exits through a narrow channel into a larger rectangular swimming pool, below. A recirculating pump keeps the water cycling between pools.

CONNECTING TO THE LAND

If you had to sum up the design philosophy of Phoenix landscape architect Christy Ten Eyck in one phrase, it might be "Honor the earth." Whether she's tackling a residential garden or a public project, using that space to reconnect people with nature is always Ten Eyck's primary aim.

Ten Eyck's love of nature developed growing up in Corsicana in southeastern Texas, a region of rolling green hills, woods, and creeks. But a rafting trip down the Grand Canyon in 1985 introduced her to another kind of natural landscape. She fell for the Southwest's austere beauty so completely during this journey that she relocated to Phoenix the following year. Ever since then, she's been teaching fellow transplants and native residents alike how to embrace rather than fight the area's climate and flora.

Here are some of the techniques Ten Eyck uses to connect her gardens with the desert beyond:

◈ MOVE OUTDOOR LIVING SPACES away from the house and closer to your property's perimeters. Tuck a new pool in among existing cactus and wildflowers, for instance. "It conveys the feeling that you have when swimming in an irrigation canal in the middle of the desert," she says.

◈ USE PERMEABLE MATERIALS like decomposed granite or gravel, which mimic the colors and textures of native soil, rather than concrete or flagstone when possible. "And go easy on the ratio of hardscape to landscape in general."

◈ MAKE THE LANDSCAPE ENGAGE all the senses. Plant for scent and movement as well as color. Add small fountains or trickling water features to delight the ear.

◈ ABOVE ALL, USE NATIVE PLANTS. Not only are they ideally suited to local soil and climate and therefore the easiest to grow and maintain, says Ten Eyck, but they also remind us of what brought us to the Southwest. "The natural beauty of the desert is still its main attraction."

A COURTYARD IS A TRANSITIONAL SPACE. ENCLOSED BY WALLS, IT'S PART GARDEN, PART HOUSE, OFFERING PRIVACY, OPEN AIR, PLANTINGS, AND FURNISHINGS.

courtyards

In New Mexico, courtyards were often called *placitas* (little plazas), and haciendas were organized around them. Similar patios distinguish Spanish missions such as San José de Tumacácori, near Tubac in southern Arizona, and San Xavier del Bac—the White Dove of the Desert—near Tucson.

Garden fragrances and breezes swirl through a courtyard to remind you that you're not indoors. A trickling fountain of some sort is a common feature, as is perhaps a shapely corner fireplace for warmth on chilly evenings. You may use a graceful palo verde or mesquite tree for shade; saltillo tiles, decomposed granite, or flagstone underfoot; pots of colorful flowers; and a bench or comfortable chairs for relaxing. Cool shadows play across the surrounding walls and let the house breathe on hot summer days.

A courtyard is a decompression zone between indoors and the outside world, offering a changeable outdoor room where the action, or drowsy inaction, takes place.

above Santa Fe courtyards often feature windows to the exterior. This one brightens the wall with blue trim and shutters and a flower-filled window box.

above Water spills from a colorful mosaic sun into a semicircular pool, bringing the welcome sight and sound of its flow to cool even the hottest days. The vibrant reds and blues of the wall tiles are cleverly repeated in the foreground petunias.

facing page Thick, plastered-adobe walls and a plank entry gate show the Mexican imprint on a Moorish-Spanish courtyard design. Against this plain backdrop, an intricately patterned tile panel of stylized bouquets above the pool recalls Persian floral mosaics. A colorful cushioned bench, right, is set among pots of cheery flowers near the small pool with its vivid tile backdrop. A built-in corner planter above the tile panel hosts plantings that soften the bare walls.

above The contemporary adobe portal in pueblo style welcomes visitors to this Albuquerque courtyard. Its earth-toned walls and generous blue gate are the dominant elements in the composition; neutral greenery softens the base, while two 'Blaze' climbing roses add a decorative touch.

right Inside the courtyard, an abundant use of green conveys a sense of lushness in contrast to the hard surfaces of walls and paving. Engulfing the ramada, a Lady Banks' rose presents a blanket of yellow blossoms in early spring.

above Luxuriant green foliage provides
a refreshing change from the dry plantings
beyond the courtyard walls. Accent color
is minimal: blue larkspur, at left, and
soft carmine Jupiter's beard (*Centranthus
ruber*) on the right.

above A classic glazed blue urn set in the center of a simple circular
pool spills water from its rim into the pool. The nearby ironwork
table and chairs nestle into the greenery, suggesting a pause to
enjoy the tranquillity.

right Outside the courtyard, simplicity reigns. A fancifully decorated
jardiniere is the sole accent, incorporating a bit of the door's vivid
blue in its riotous colors.

below Massive stoneware urns with flowering century plants flank the entry to this pocket-size courtyard. Though contemporary in design, it is faithful to traditional courtyard function as an outdoor room secluded from public view.

above High walls and a carpet of gravel make this courtyard very much an open-air room. Plants in terra-cotta pots allow a decor change whenever the fancy strikes. The stone-mantled fireplace with its generous raised hearth is a powerful lure on chilly days and evenings.

below Although this courtyard is walled round, the hillside is what gives it seclusion. Mexican style is everywhere, from the tile pavement and ironwork furniture to the flourishing bougainvillea flanking the fireplace.

HIDDEN PLEASURES

The walled gardens of Santa Fe are like willful flirts. They seem to leave the shuttered windows in their thick adobe walls slightly ajar just to tease. Walking by, you catch glimpses of zinnias, marigolds, and hollyhocks reveling in patches of sun—and beyond, cool shady corners where you could find shelter from the heat. It's wonderfully alluring, and you wish you could see more.

Those thick walls are meant to protect, however, not to tempt. Gardening within enclosures just makes sense in this beautiful but harsh environment. In summer, the walls give shade to plants and people. In winter, the heat they absorb provides warmth. Within walls, plants are less easily desiccated by dry winds or pelted with hail. Rabbits and other hungry marauders are kept out, too.

Because walled courtyards are basically outdoor rooms, much space is given up to activities for people, like dining and napping. Planting is relatively spare, but, to compensate, flower color is often intense—shades such as hot pink, chile red, and pumpkin orange, which can stand up to strong sun. Shutters and doors are painted vividly, too, most characteristically deep blue. Wooden tables and chairs are painted other hues, and multicolored Mexican folk art adds a final splash.

There's a lot we can learn from these flirts. Wrangle an invitation inside the walls during your next visit to Santa Fe.

An openwork gate panel allows tantalizing glimpses into this courtyard, but strategically placed interior walls preserve privacy. Agaves are featured plants, their sculptural forms creating living art in a minimalist setting.

EVERY TIME THE SOUTHWEST FACES A SERIOUS DROUGHT, GARDENERS REDISCOVER INDIGENOUS PLANTS AND WATER-SAVING LANDSCAPE DESIGNS.

waterwise gardens

When the drought danger passes, we're tempted to go back to our old habits. But savvy gardeners understand that, in this arid region, droughts can hang around for years, and prolonged hot dry weather is a fact of life. They know that dry landscapes make sense.

"Dry" doesn't have to mean cacti alone: many kinds of trees, shrubs, vines, and ground covers, introduced from dry climates throughout the world (including Mexico, Baja, and our own Southwest deserts), need little water once established. What these tough but showy plants have in common is their ability to handle the extreme heat, low humidity, high winds, and alkaline soils typical of arid climates.

A waterwise garden relies mostly on such plants to achieve year-round color, texture, and form; it confines any thirsty plants (including lawn) to a small "mini-oasis" near the house. Decomposed granite or pavers serve as ground covers of choice, with drifts of low, mounding plants such as verbena, lippia, or *Aptenia* 'Red Apple' as accents.

As a waterwise gardener, you can harvest rainwater from summer monsoons. Form berms to direct and hold water around trees, channel roof runoff into large barrels for watering potted plants, install efficient irrigation systems (drip systems work well), and group plants by their water needs.

facing page Desert native plants offer the ultimate in drought tolerance. Spiky yuccas, symmetrical barrel cacti, and rushlike lady's slipper (*Pedilanthus macrocarpus*) make sculptural statements; purple verbena provides color.

below To compensate for the Southwest's harsh conditions, this garden in Phoenix is sited on the house's east side—a better location for growing flowers. Purple irises, red snapdragons, and rosy penstemons add punch to oasis-style beds. Paths of decomposed granite mimic the desert floor. An orchard of citrus and fruit trees grows behind, against the backdrop of Camelback Mountain.

right Luxuriant flowers—purple moss verbena and pink penstemon—belie the fact that this is a waterwise landscape. All the plants take full sun, heat, and only moderate water. As a bonus, a number of them are attractive to birds—encouraging them to linger a while.

left In high desert and mountain gardens, nothing beats two perennial prairie daisies for reliability with little care. Purple coneflower (*Echinacea purpurea*) comes in pink shades, purple, and white; gloriosa daisy (*Rudbeckia hirta*) claims the warm hues from yellow through orange to brown.

facing page Thirsty plants are set in containers and concentrated in one area for easy watering. This courtyard pool ringed with potted petunias is a good example of waterwise Old World tradition transported to arid regions of Mexico and the Southwest.

SMART OASES
In Southwest gardens, an oasis is quite different from the Hollywood movie set vision of palm-fringed pools surrounded by endless shifting sands. Here, an oasis is a small greenbelt hugging the house where you concentrate water use on container plants, treasured tropicals, and perhaps a tiny lawn. You spend most of your water budget in this oasis, since it is the part of the garden that's most heavily used. Then you choose unthirsty plants for other areas.

Just beyond the oasis is a compromise zone for moderate water users—plants that grow and look best with deep irrigations five times a year or so. Choose these plants to blend with those naturally occurring in the desert beyond. On the property's perimeter, nature takes over. Plants in this zone require little or no water beyond that provided by earth and atmosphere. Leave native vegetation where you find it, and scatter wildflower seeds for winter and spring color.

Oases are used throughout the Southwest, but especially in Tucson, where water supplies come almost entirely from groundwater. If you live in an urban area, your garden might have room for only one zone beyond your oasis.

SOME OF THE MOST BEAUTIFUL PLANTS IN THE SOUTHWEST GROW HERE NATURALLY, AND THEY HAVE EVOLVED TO THRIVE IN ARIDITY AND ROUGH SOILS.

native gardens

A native plant garden makes good use of the best indigenous varieties, with beguiling names like fairy duster and Apache plume, tufted evening primrose and Mexican hat. Casual in style, a design of natives consumes little in the way of water or maintenance time.

To reestablish a bit of the desert around your home, put in fast-growing native flowering plants; then let them evolve naturally, perhaps helping them along with a little thinning and watering. Once established, many native shrubs, perennials, and wildflowers reseed themselves, creating a colorful garden that changes year after year. And they can provide food and cover for desert birds such as cactus wrens and verdins.

Truly wild gardens may not suit every gardener or neighborhood; they're most at home near the desert's edge. But a slightly more organized version based on native plants can work wonderfully in urban settings.

above Desert beard tongue (*Penstemon pseudospectabilis*).

right Penstemania! Dry regions of the West and Southwest abound in native penstemons, all of which offer plenty of color on easy-growing plants. This spring-time display features pink flowers of *Penstemon parryi* and *P. pseudospectabilis*; firecracker penstemon, *P. eatonii*, supplies the red.

above In the low desert, "go with the flow" means using heat- and drought-tolerant natives. In this artful garden, a handsome palo verde tree contributes height to a planting of yellow desert marigolds, assorted cacti (prickly pear, organ-pipe, barrel), and two different agaves.

left Desert marigold (*Baileya multiradiata*) ranks high among waterwise Southwest perennials. It blooms from spring into fall—even through winter in the warmest regions.

NATURALLY SOUTHWEST

For Ron Gass, native plants are simply the best. "When the palo verdes bloom and the fairy dusters are in flower, it's pretty glorious here," he says. Gass first became smitten with plants that grow naturally in the desert when, as a young horticulture student at the University of Arizona, he frequently encountered native plants in his favorite class, plant taxonomy. After college and a brief stint growing natives for the Arizona Department of Transportation to plant along the state's freeways, he and his wife, Maureen, opened their Mountain States Wholesale Nursery, in Glendale, Arizona. They focused at first on Southwest natives.

A chance meeting with Greg Starr (who later opened a retail nursery in Tucson) led to an ongoing partnership in plant exploration. In 1986, the two made their first trip to the Chihuahuan desert in northeastern Mexico in search of dry-climate plants. Since then, they've combed the deserts—and the world—with Maureen and Greg's wife, Carol, in search of beautiful, garden-friendly plants that like desert conditions.

Why should we care about native and desert-adapted plants? Because water is precious here, and droughts are a fact of life, explains Gass. Also because development is a constant threat to the fragile desert ecosystems. "The desert is so beautiful; we shouldn't impose our way of life on it," says Gass. "Instead, we should learn to incorporate our way of living into the desert. We should appreciate and live with it." For gardeners new to the desert who are used to the lawns and greenery of wetter climates, Gass suggests a visit to the Desert Botanical Garden in Phoenix "to see what can be done."

Native plants are increasingly the plants of choice here. "The look of Phoenix has changed in the past 30 years," says Gass. "Palo verdes and other natives have taken the place of mulberries and ash trees."

Among Gass's favorite plants are Angelita daisy (shown above), "a wonderful little plant" with yellow blooms, and 'New Gold' lantana, which is "not native, but it stands up well in heat and adds pizzazz to the summer landscape."

Greg and Carol Starr join Maureen and Ron Gass (*right*) on a collection trip in the Southwest desert. To preserve native plant populations in the wild, pioneers such as the Gasses and the Starrs gather only seeds or cuttings, never plants. Collecting any plant material in the wild is best left to professionals.

A DRAMATIC NATURAL LANDSCAPE OF BUTTES AND MESAS, ROCK WASHES
AND PALM-SHADED CANYONS IS THE PERFECT FOIL FOR THE BOLDLY DESIGNED
HOUSE AND GARDEN.

sculptural gardens

Cacti and succulents such as agave and yucca are the Southwest garden's indisputable stars; their bold, architectural shapes are living sculptures that complement the sleek, clean lines of a contemporary home.

The fountainlike, arching leaves of a trio of octopus agaves can mask and soften a low wall's somewhat harsh angles. Desert spoon (*Dasylirion wheeleri*), a native plant that forms mounds of spiky blue-green foliage,

can accentuate a gently curving path. Drifts of bunny ears (*Opuntia microdasys*) are bold accents against clumps of feathery deer grass. An organpipe cactus can stand sentinel beside a purple-flowered flow of *Verbena rigida*.

Position boldly shaped plants where their forms show off best and their shadows fall across paving and walls. Put stiff, upright chollas and saguaros where they capture backlighting from the sun or are lit from below by lamps. To enhance the drama, group plants by kind—a wide swath of barrel cacti interspersed here and there with clusters of ocotillo, for instance, or saguaros of varying heights marching across a long, narrow planting bed.

Other elements that can add drama to the sculptural garden are built rather than grown: chunky wing walls painted in rich colors; spheres or triangles of concrete that add interest to pools of decomposed granite. The look is simple, dramatic, bold.

Plant combinations can make striking sculptural statements. In this garden in Paradise Valley, Arizona, massed plantings of *Aloe vera* thrust narrow leaves and slim flower spikes upward, contrasting with barrel cacti and clumps of lavender cotton (*Santolina chamaecyparissus*). Atop two pillars, potted fine-textured *Agave geminiflora* forms round foliage fountains.

right In this Santa Fe garden, lush cottonwood trees and a long black fountain preside over an entry courtyard; potted red geraniums act as accents.

facing page Modern and minimalist—intersecting, unadorned rectangular walls offer a "museum" setting for the art of similarly spare yuccas. Their carefully groomed thick trunks have been shorn of foliage save for crowns of stiff, silvery leaves.

above A steely blue-gray *Agave weberi* adds fountainlike punch to a tangle of relaxed, shrubby plants in this Tucson garden. Closer to the house, a date palm (*Phoenix dactylifera*) spreads feathery foliage atop its stout trunk.

right An Egyptian-style palm frond motif graces a handsome ironwork gate and the light fixtures on either side, with a variant in a sculpture to the right. Beneath the lights, two potted sago palms (*Cycas revoluta*) reinforce the theme.

below *E pluribus unum*—from many plants, one piece of sculpture. A clay bowl hosts cacti and succulents in an array of styles: columnar, rosette-form, and jointed flat pads.

right More spines than plant, one diminutive hedgehog cactus (*Echinocereus fendleri*) can be a simple sculpture. Disproportionately large flowers add a touch of whimsy.

above An assembly of stone monoliths forms a backyard sculpture garden reminiscent of Stonehenge or Easter Island. The tallest stones reach seven feet, rising from a sea of decomposed granite. Blooming lavender spikes and silvery hummocks of white-flowered bush morning glory (*Convolvulus cneorum*) break the bare expanse.

above Organpipe cactus (*Stenocereus thurberi*) offers more than sculptural columns with spiny ribs. On spring evenings, you can look forward to pink-blushed white blossoms.

above In a low desert garden of citrus and shrubs, native cacti and succulents are scattered about for contrast. Jointed pads of spineless prickly pear cactus (*Opuntia ficus-indica*) dance in the foreground; rosettes of swordlike agave leaves nestle in the background gravel.

right If you lack water, go for illusion! This broad expanse of flagstone is unexpectedly bisected by a flowing faux stream. Its meandering course of blue stones cleverly breaks paving monotony—and, of course, conserves water.

With a careful arrangement of plants, you can turn a landscape into a living-sculpture garden. In this Las Vegas front yard, purple prickly pear (*Opuntia violacea santa-rita*), bare-stemmed ocotillo (*Fouquieria splendens*), deer grass (*Muhlenbergia rigens*), and desert spoon (*Dasylirion wheeleri*) are grouped as they appear in nature.

A rivulet of water meanders down the center of this sculptural banquet table and empties into a splash pool. The flagstone shapes of the tabletop appear to have risen from the pavement below.

IN THE ROCKY, SCRUBBY SONORAN DESERT THAT SPRAWLS ACROSS
SOUTHERN ARIZONA AND INTO NORTHERN MEXICO THE SAGUARO
IS KING.

saguaro country

As you crunch your way up the hilly trail in the soft dawn light, silhouettes of giant saguaros rise around you. Strangely human, they seem to hold their arms skyward, wave them, or reach out to neighboring saguaros in a kind of freeze-frame dance. Between

them, palo verdes spread bony green limbs topped with fine clouds of yellow blooms. Calls of flickers, quail, and cactus wrens float across the chilly air, and off to the south a pair of coyotes move out of the valley and over the ridge.

More than any other plants, the saguaros that grow here by the hundreds of thousands define this landscape. Their fruits nourish insects, birds, and bats and have provided generations of native peoples with tasty harvests. Their hulking frames shelter a rich diversity of animals and birds. Gila woodpeckers and gilded flickers excavate nest holes in them, raise their young, and then move on. The walls of their holes callus, leaving relatively cool, well-insulated spaces that owls can take over. Cactus wrens, white-winged doves, and red-tailed hawks build nests in the crotches between arms and trunk. And after a big plant drops fruits in early summer, an array of animals from javelinas (peccaries) and coyotes to birds move in to feast, dispersing seed in the process.

left In a contemporary art display, four Argentine saguaros (*Trichocereus terscheckii*) congregate as living sculpture against a wall painted deep eggplant. Ground-level lights shining against the wall create dramatic shadows at night.

left A pillar of its garden community, this solitary saguaro stands sentinel over an assortment of desert companions. The constriction in its trunk is permanent evidence of a few lean years in the plant's past. At this size and age, the trunk is ready to initiate armlike branches.

below A downward-curving limb provides a rare close-up view of the saguaro's waxlike blossoms (the state flower of Arizona). Edible red fruits will follow these nectar-rich blooms. Neatly framed between trunk and branch is a husky mature saguaro.

The seeds germinate and take root beneath palo verde or mesquite trees, where they find shelter from sun, wind, and small gnawing animals. They grow very slowly to 50 feet tall, putting out their first flowers when they're about 60 years old, and living 150 to 200 years.

The saguaro (*Carnegiea gigantea*) is a protected species. When buying a mature specimen, be sure it was collected legally. When choosing a nursery-grown plant, look for one with a good root system. Give these plants excellent drainage.

Like all cacti, saguaros are accent pieces; give them room so that you can appreciate them individually. Observe how they grow in the wild—singly or in well-spaced clusters, among palo verdes or low shrubs, rocky mulch and boulders—and then duplicate the look. Or plant several in a row against a backdrop of solid-color walls, to highlight their elegant forms.

A FANTASY GARDEN IS INSPIRED BY YOUR IMAGINATION, BY MEMORIES OF PLACES
YOU'VE BEEN, OR BY VISIONS OF PLACES YOU LONG TO VISIT. IT CAN CAPTURE
THE SPIRIT OF A DISTANT LAND.

fantasy gardens

Close your eyes, and transport yourself to the place of your dreams.
What does your garden escape look like? Is it a palm-shaded
canyon oasis with a Moroccan-style pavilion, or a colorful Mexican
resort with thatch-roofed *palapas* dotted around an azure swimming pool? Maybe it's a favorite hiking place—Sabino Canyon just north
of Tucson in the Santa Catalina Mountains, for instance—with sculpted
boulders and a waterfall coursing down the rocks. Or a marketplace in
southern France, where colorful umbrellas spread a vibrant canopy over
plazas bursting with activity.

Now get more specific. Are the paths through your garden to be made
of Arizona flagstone, decomposed granite, or saltillo tiles? Is your fantasia
to be surrounded by walls, fences, or hedges? Are there fountains, gazebos,
arbors, or dining pavilions in the picture? What are the predominant
flower and fabric colors? Which plants can enhance the look while thriving
in the southwestern soil and climate? What style are the furnishings and
accessories? Write down your ideas. Save clippings and photos of designs
you like. Then make sure they all work together to create the effect you
want before you dig in to make your dream garden a reality.

top This garden re-creates the mood of a desert oasis. Water spills from a boulder-rimmed spring
into a pond. The island bed in the foreground, surrounded with Arizona flagstone, is planted with
cactus, purple verbena, and yellow Angelita daisies.

EVEN IF YOUR BACKYARD IS ABOUT THE SIZE AND SHAPE OF A TWO-CAR GARAGE (AS MANY ARE IN NEW DEVELOPMENTS), YOU CAN CREATE TONS OF AMBIANCE.

small gardens

It's possible to turn an uninspired little rectangle of concrete into an inviting outdoor room by adding a dynamic water feature, multiple conversation areas, and layered plantings to provide privacy around the periphery. A small garden needs a focal point, especially if it has no sweeping vistas over the back wall. A small pond or fountain set in a corner of the yard, with a shapely boulder or two behind it to draw your eye there, can serve this purpose. A comfortable bench (or a table and chairs)—whether on a small satellite patio near the back fence with a path leading to it or on a paved area just outside the back door—is another important element.

In tiny spaces, poor-quality materials can be painfully evident, so splurge on the best pavers, tiles, and other hardscape elements you can afford. Simplify your plantings by keeping the color scheme restrained and the plants in scale with the space. Soften peripheral walls with vines, and put compact shrubs in front of them for a layered effect.

To make your garden appear larger, orient your paths, patios, and plantings on the diagonal, or incorporate the view beyond your wall into your design.

above A pueblo-style home has planting pockets sparingly adorned with prickly pear cacti, purple fountain grass, and santolina. The rainfall-collecting dry creek bed beside it runs under the bridge leading to the gate; it keeps runoff from draining toward the house. Bougainvillea drapes the wall behind.

right A medley of color marks this small front entry garden. Magenta-flowered *Calandrinia spectabilis*, gold-and-rust gaillardia 'Goblin', 'Cherry Meidiland' shrub roses, and tall kangaroo paws ('Bush Sunset' and 'Yellow Gem') make this a sidewalk showstopper. The secrets of its success are heat tolerance and a modest need for water.

facing page Berm plantings—including native blue *Yucca rigida*, yellow-flowered brittlebush (*Encelia farinosa*), indigo bush, and a palo brea tree—flank this sinuous path in Phoenix to provide the house with a measure of privacy. The arbor creates a shady outdoor living area.

right In the patio shown on this page, blue tiles form the fireplace hearth and a built-in *banco* seating area to its left; they are repeated in a horizontal band where the chimney narrows. On the mantel, a wrought-iron wall sculpture and an array of candles provide more regional touches beneath a sun disk.

below With the world shut out behind thick walls, who wouldn't want to take advantage of these two inviting chaises? A multihued umbrella offers warm-season relief, while planting pockets and a blue-glazed pot add softening sprays of greenery.

above Solid patio walls are decorated by colorful panels of stacked roofing tiles. And the spaces between tiles let breezes filter through, helping cool the area whenever the air stirs.

left Designed for mounting on a flat surface, this ceramic container holds aloft a flaming red impatiens attached like a living corsage to the blue-violet stucco wall.

below Another corner of the garden boasts a riotous display of potted annuals (nasturtiums, petunias), plus a red-painted basket and a squash-blossom-yellow rocker. The floral print fabric of the chair's seat cushion adds more flowers to the scene.

A GARDEN NEEDS A QUIET NOOK WHERE YOU CAN RELAX, PUT THE CARES OF
THE DAY BEHIND YOU, AND FIND PEACE AND TRANQUILLITY.

retreats

If it is small enough, your entire garden can be a sanctuary; you may need to surround it with trees, pillowy shrubs, or walls to give it privacy from neighboring houses. But a remote corner of the garden—away from such activity hubs as the dining terrace, the firepit, and the play areas and sheltered from street noise and a neighbor's buzzing pool pump—is the perfect spot for a personal hideaway.

Orient your retreat to face a great view of the desert or mountains or to capture the sunrise or sunset. Then make the space your own. Enclose it with a hedge or vine-covered trellis. Furnish it for comfort, with a daybed or lounging chair and a scattering of colorful cushions. Set out candles or lanterns for soft evening light. Fill pots with fragrant flowers such as cottage pinks, stock, gardenias, or orange jessamine, whose blossoms will perfume the air around you and provide aromatherapy for free. To delight your senses, bring in a few things you love: a favorite sculpture, mementos of your travels, a piece of bark or a basket of stones picked up on a hike. Add a tabletop fountain for a little water music. Then relax, and allow your soul to bloom.

facing page Color is a key element in establishing the mood of a garden. This secluded, restful patio niche invites relaxation with its tasseled hammock in shades of blue. The contrasting terra-cotta backdrop adds sheltering warmth to the picture.

right A feline advance guard checks out a table for three. Simple café furniture outfits a small, gravel-surfaced garden alcove. Secluded by a fringe of desert-native plants, it suggests relaxing conversation over a spot of iced tea.

below The shell of a ruined Old West building is reborn as a rustic retreat. Massive new overhead beams give a sense of shelter; the added brick support pillar rises from flooring of the same material. Leather *equipale* chairs, two clay vessels, and a terra-cotta wall plaque suffice as adornment.

right Southwest style and building materials join forces in this elevated patio just made for evening entertaining. The arc-shaped *banco* (bench) repeats the adobe look of the garden's walls, while native stones construct the pavement, fireplace, and even the rugged coffee table.

below Montane forest embraces a patio designed to mimic a clearing in the woods. Native materials are the key. Stones from the site were used for the curved retaining wall, the patio pavers and accent boulders; native plants spill into the area, linking it to the surrounding greenery.

Featuring both furniture and potted geraniums, this covered alcove porch forms a transitional space between house and garden. The centerpiece chaise, adorned with a steer-head pillow and fabric in a regional design motif, offers comfortable relaxation away from the vagaries of the weather.

A slightly elevated pocket-size patio appears to float in a junglelike garden of luxuriant foliage. Outfitted with wrought-iron table and chairs, it invites you to step outside and relax over morning tea or coffee in a fantasy tropical world defying the desert.

A NATURAL-LOOKING GARDEN SUBTLY BLENDS ELEMENTS THAT LOOK AS THOUGH THEY WERE LIFTED FROM THE SOUTHWEST'S MAJESTIC WILD LANDSCAPE.

naturalistic gardens

In desert areas, clusters of cacti and palo verde trees might borrow the native landscape beyond the garden's boundaries for a backdrop. Sand-colored boulders anchor the plantings. Plants are arranged in groups as they would grow naturally on wildland. In higher elevations, wildflowers can create a spatter-paint effect among grasses and tall pines.

If you choose to have a water feature, make it irregular in shape and nestle it like a natural spring among small boulders or feathery grasses.

Avoid hard edges; make your paths curved.

Naturalistic gardens make the most of what nature provides, whether shades of beige and silvery gray-green, or frost-browned grasses, or sculptural pines that make striking accents against billowy white storm clouds. They incorporate the plants that grow naturally in the Southwest, including saguaros, palo verdes, chollas, opuntias. A "naturally Southwest" garden celebrates our native landscape in its many gorgeous shades.

A rocky dry streambed winds its way through a low desert landscape thick with native plants. Massed beavertail cacti crowd the stream's upper edge, their oval gray pads echoing the shape and color of the stones. Overhead, gnarly palo verde stems dispense a filmy spray of yellow blossoms.

above The stout saguaro and the brush-shaped Joshua tree tell you that you're in the Sonoran Desert. A variety of colorful desert plants, including yellow desert marigold, sky-blue desert bluebells, and pink- and scarlet-flowered penstemons, accompany these two signature natives.

left A naturalistic planting island fronts this Spanish-colonial house. Among the plants are a yellow-flowered sweet acacia tree (*Acacia farnesiana*), pink Parry's penstemon, and yellow Angelita daisy. Steely blue *Agave americana* adds a bold accent.

below The "old watering hole" is as appealing to these goats as to swimmers. In the Texas scene here and at right, the pool underlines an oak and the natural vista beyond.

above Why bother to landscape too much when nature does it so well? This Texas home, designed for interaction with the out-of-doors, sits on a plateau among natural boulders, a grove of live oaks, and assorted low-growing native plants.

below A brick-edged gravel path winds through a Phoenix front-yard garden of bird- and butterfly-friendly native plants. Mesquite and palo verde trees offer height and shade; shrubs include brittlebush, hop bush, and *Salvia greggii*. Native annual wildflowers and African daisies make a splash in spring.

above To achieve this effect, nature needed a helping hand—but the scene looks natural. The existing cacti, trees, and shrubs were augmented by a lavish sowing of assorted native wildflower seeds; with judicious watering, the result is a "desert in spring" landscape.

right Effective landscapes don't require an endless variety of countless plants. Here, a re-created dry wash flows through a gravelly desert of artfully placed boulders, cacti, and native shrubs. Not only does the planting look natural, but it also is adapted to the area's climate.

This Palm Desert land-scape relies on plants native to the Sonoran Desert. Clumps of bunny ears cactus dominate, interspersed with silvery gray mounds of brittle-bush and furry-looking deer grass. Two young saguaro cacti rise in the background, while two different palo verde trees add height.

Picturesque gnarled branches of an old mesquite tree set the tone for a Tucson garden of regional native plants arrayed in naturalistic style. Prominent are pink blossoms of globe mallow and penstemon; annual wildflowers provide varied spots of color in winter and spring.

ORNAMENTAL GRASSES

Grasses dot every part of the Southwest landscape; no wonder they fit so naturally into local gardens. They soften the hardscape, extend the palette of plant colors and textures, and put up airy flower heads that dance in the late-summer breeze. Many of the region's best grasses are American natives, unfazed by heat and drought—some even offer fall color. Twenty years ago, few native grasses were available to gardeners, but in the past decade designers, gardeners, and nursery people have learned their worth.

For impact, use big bluestem (*Andropogon gerardii*), the mainstay of the tall-grass prairies. It grows 3 to 8 feet tall, depending on summer water, and the leaves are infused with maroon in fall.

Three tall native muhly grasses are also dramatic: bamboo muhly grass (*Muhlenbergia dumosa*) has the look of a 3- to 6-foot-tall bamboo (taller with extra summer water); *M. lindheimeri* sends amber flower spikes above its 5-foot mound of foliage; and deer grass (*M. rigens*) makes a dense, 4-foot-tall backbone plant, with yellow or purplish flower spikes emerging in late summer.

Among switch grasses, *Panicum virgatum* 'Prairie Sky' has the bluest leaves; it grows 5 feet tall and 3 feet wide. Adapted exotics include dwarf pampas grass (*Cortaderia selloana* 'Pumila'), about 6 feet tall, with a long season of huge white plumes; it tolerates alkaline soil, and this dwarf doesn't usually set seed.

For smaller spaces, make a shortgrass prairie by mixing 'Hatchita' blue grama (*Bouteloua gracilis*) or 'Sea Urchin' blue fescue (*Festuca glauca*) with low-growing desert wildflowers.

To have something at least knee-high and drought tolerant, try blue oat grass (*Helictotrichon sempervirens*), which looks like a larger version of blue fescue, or 'Nashville' purple muhly (*M. rigida*), with its true purple flower spikes. For intensely blue leaves that age to coppery purple in autumn, plant 'The Blues' little bluestem (*Schizachyrium scoparium*, often sold as *Andropogon scoparius*). Its seedheads color in fall.

By far the most graceful native grass is Mexican feather grass (*Nassella tenuissima*, often still sold as *Stipa tenuissima*), a 2-foot elegant fountain. Its alternative common name, angel hair grass, describes it better after its chartreuse new growth fades to straw color.

Blue oat grass (*Helictotrichon sempervirens*).

IT'S EASY TO TURN YOUR GARDEN INTO A SANCTUARY FOR A VARIETY OF CREATURES, WINGED AND WILD, IF YOU GIVE THEM WHAT THEY NEED.

wildlife gardens

A backyard wildlife habitat is alive with beauty and motion. Hummingbirds perform aerial acrobatics over the blossoms; chirping sounds and birdsong fill the air. Butterflies bask on sun-warmed rocks. To draw wildlife to your garden, bring in trees and shrubs that offer shelter and nesting sites; for additional cover provide hollow logs, stacked rocks, and woodpiles, which are perfect hiding places for lizards, quail, rabbits, and other small animals. Set out food plants whose berries, foliage, fruit, nectar, nuts, pollen, sap, and seeds create a living smorgasbord at which different critters can dine on what they like in peace; combine plants that bloom at different times of the year to keep the feast going. And provide year-round sources of water for bathing and sipping by installing ponds or birdbaths (the trickling sound of a water drip or fountain enhances the attraction).

Avoid using toxic chemicals in the garden; they can harm or kill the wildlife you're trying to attract. Insects, after all, provide food for birds, toads, and other animals.

Your backyard wildlife habitat can help the many creatures whose native habitats are disappearing as housing and commercial developments encroach on wildlands. And, in return, you can enjoy the pleasures of viewing wildlife up close.

above Black-chinned hummingbird (*Archilochus alexandri*).

right Desert denizens love this garden. Native and other drought-tolerant plants offer a variety of foods and habitats for birds and small animals (note the rabbit). Blossoms of red *Salvia greggii* and orange *Aloe saponaria* are guaranteed magnets for any hummingbirds in the vicinity.

HUMMINGBIRDS

The Southwest is hummingbird country. In late winter, most species migrate out of Mexico in search of flower-rich breeding grounds to the north; they start their journey by following ocotillo and *Justicia* bloom as it moves across the southwestern desert.

Look closely around your garden: you may find one of the birds' egg-cup nests—often in some precarious, fairly public spot like the top of a ripening orange. Hummingbirds make five or six feeding forays per hour; between forays, males usually go to a lookout perch, occasionally buzzing out to defend their territory from other hummers.

How do these birds captivate us so completely? Maybe it's their size: some are hardly bigger than moths. Or their in-flight aerobics: they can rocket straight up, swoop straight down, fly backward or upside down, and hover with ease, outmaneuvering anything else in the sky. As avian top guns that regularly pick off insects in midflight, they're natural weapons in a gardener's arsenal.

To invite hummingbirds into your garden, set out plants whose nectar-rich blooms attract them, such as bougainvillea, California fuchsia, chuparosa, lemon bottlebrush, ocotillo, some penstemons, *Salvia greggii*, or shrimp plant (*Justicia brandegeeana*). In winter, try hanging up a feeder or two. Fill the feeders with a nectar that's almost identical to what they'd find in the wild: mix 1 part white granulated sugar with 4 parts water; boil for 2 minutes, cool to room temperature, and then pour into the feeder. Replace your mixture weekly, and wash all the feeder parts.

right In desert regions, what is more alluring than water? Birdbaths always tempt avian visitors like this dove for bathing and drinking. Be sure the water is shallow enough for their feet to touch bottom, and place baths near bushy plants that offer refuge.

CARE OF THE TORTOISE

Although it is illegal to remove desert tortoises from the wild, the animals already in captivity often need new homes. Since they can live for more than 100 years, they sometimes simply outlive their owners. You can "adopt" a tortoise (serve as its custodian), though the animals remain the property of the state of Arizona. To find out what's involved in taking care of them, contact the Arizona-Sonora Desert Museum (an approved adoption agency) at www.desertmuseum.org.

above, top In a perfect alliance of plant and animal, an owl views the world from its hideaway (originally hollowed out by wood-peckers) in a mature saguaro. This cool refuge is entirely harmless to the saguaro.

above, bottom Nectar-rich flowers are guaranteed to attract assorted butterflies. This painted lady eagerly extracts the precious fluid from a desert native groundsel (*Senecio*).

GARDENS AND ENTERTAINING GO TOGETHER. GUESTS LOVE TO MINGLE IN THE OPEN AIR IN EYE-PLEASING SETTINGS WITH COMFORTABLE FURNISHINGS.

entertaining gardens

What makes some landscapes work better for entertaining than others? Wide paths, spacious patios, and abundant outdoor seating, for starters. You want your guests to be able to move easily through your garden and to feel comfortable when they're seated or dining.

Other elements that set the scene for fun and good conversation include soft lighting, fountains, firepits, pools, game courts, and visual surprises, such as whimsical garden art tucked among foliage.

A garden designed for entertaining has outdoor cooking facilities of some sort—a freestanding barbecue for grilling a few steaks, an open firepit

for toasting marshmallows or hot dogs, or a fully stocked outdoor kitchen with refrigerator, sink, and built-in pizza oven or wok. Let your budget and the amount and type of entertaining you do determine the kind of outdoor kitchen you install. Position the cooking area near an entrance to your indoor kitchen for easy transport of food and utensils.

For dining, set aside a paved area that's lightly shaded from the hottest sun by trees or structures such as ramadas. If possible, locate it near an outdoor fireplace or firepit to take the chill off the evening air. Choose a sturdy table and comfortable chairs.

To enhance the outdoor dining experience, place pots filled with perfumed flowers nearby. Use candles or luminarias to supplement permanent lighting, or string little white lights on a patio arbor. Scatter colorful pillows on seat walls. Then let the party begin.

above A spacious covered porch, conceived in the style of old Mexican haciendas, offers a restful gathering place as well as a great viewing platform from which to appreciate an expansive desert vista. Easy access to the swimming pool makes it the perfect drying-off spot between dips.

right This alfresco dining area incorporates views of the outlying desert. A full-scale, permanent kitchen contains everything needed to put on a banquet, including generous counter space.

facing page Gracious outdoor dining takes place beneath an impressive pergola tucked into a sheltered alcove. Cascading vines spread foliage traceries over concrete walls, softening their hard surface and giving a hint of the garden beyond.

Four comfortable chairs create a conversation grouping where guests can assemble in the cool of a desert evening around a chill-dispelling fire. Any hardier souls who fancy an evening dip in the pool will find that it's just the spot for a quick après-swim warm-up.

This sheltered patio abuts an inviting swimming pool, the two ingeniously linked by a raised spa straddling the edge that separates them. After a relaxing soak and a lap or two in the pool, the family can anticipate a light repast by a cozy fire beneath the vine-draped pergola.

All set up for stress reduction, this Tucson-area patio provides a swimmin' hole–size pool for getting the kinks out and a row of comfortable chaises in which to kick back afterward. Entertainment comes from watching the play of light and shadow on the desert and hills beyond.

above A hillside entertainment area
affords a sweeping vista of Palm
Springs–area mountains from either
pool or fireside. The spacious fireplace
delivers serious warmth on chilly
evenings—often after having produced
a seriously large barbecue feast.

right Come sit *here!* Eye-popping red
paint leaves no doubt where to find
bench seating in this Phoenix patio.
Assorted throw pillows featuring Native
American design motifs are provided to
soften the hard surfaces.

above This small soaking pool, glimpsed in the photo at left, is fed by a water channel recessed in the top of a curved retaining wall that outlines the spacious seating area on a higher level. Entering the pool in a precise waterfall, the water recirculates through a paving-level drain.

right Here are all the comforts of home, but—believe it or not—outdoors! This irresistible lounging bed tucks into an ell of the house where it is sheltered from the elements by the two house walls and a broad roof overhang. To the left, atop the stonework, is a convenient wet bar.

IN THE FOOTHILLS OF NEW MEXICO'S SANGRE DE CRISTO MOUNTAINS OR HIGH
ABOVE PALM SPRINGS IN IDYLLWILD, GARDENS HAVE THEIR OWN DISTINCTIVE STYLES.

higher-elevation
gardens

Surrounded by pine forests and a rolling landscape of arroyos and canyons, mountain landscapes are often rugged and rustic. Boulders are accents; peeled poles or prunings make fences and arbors.

Though growing seasons are shorter here, gardeners find plenty of reasons to celebrate the beauty outside their doors: summer flowers whose colors blaze brighter in the crystalline air; aspen trees that flicker in the slightest breeze and turn brilliant yellow in fall; snow that dusts the trees and grasses with white in winter.

Gardening in this climate can be challenging. But you can take your design cues from nature. Plan your landscape for all-season interest—columbines, lilacs and lupines, peonies and poppies for spring bloom; coneflowers, goldenrods, and sunflowers for summer bloom. Duplicate the look of plantings that grow wild nearby, the pillowy asters that thread their way through grasses or chamisa against a backdrop of boulders.

It's a different world up high, where white clouds billow across electric blue skies, and juniper and piñon smoke scents the air on cold nights. Few mountain gardeners would trade it for any place on earth.

The weathered-wood gate and pueblo-influenced home style suggest the Southwest, but the brick paving, lawn, and green backdrop could pass for a *North*west setting. That's the high-elevation difference: more moisture, more greenery.

above This Santa Fe home and its garden mesh seamlessly with the surrounding natural terrain. The native boulders both define and accent planting areas where natives like prominent blue oat grass mingle with a varied assortment of low-growing and shrubby non-natives suited to the climate.

right Elsewhere in the same Santa Fe garden, a procession of stone steps winds uphill, past a lawn plateau, to its ultimate destination: a hot tub with a dramatic, full-circle view. The entire area is conceived as a gigantic rock garden, native and exotic plants springing up in the crevices.

above In the high country,
summer shade gives relief from
the heat. But when winter snow
and cold arrive, sunshine
becomes a welcome commodity.
Deciduous trees can address
the issue: their leaves shade the
house from spring through
summer, and then drop in fall
to let winter sun shine in.

right Rustic stone—plentiful in
the high country—provides building material perfectly attuned to
the site; blue window trim lends
a special Southwest accent. An
antique farm cart now serves as
garden decor, hauling a load
of pink blossoms.

above This front courtyard in Santa Fe differs from its lowland counterparts. Here, the landscape features shrubs and perennials with moderate water needs (including lavender, lamb's ears, and creeping thyme); a dry faux streambed and the stone pathway divide the plantings into island beds.

right The centerpiece of this garden, north of Taos, is a free-form, natural-looking pond. Regional stones outline its perimeter, while water-thrifty perennials, such as purple-flowered Russian sage, hot-pink ice plant, and white-flowered *Datura inoxia*, crowd in from all sides. Two biofilters keep the water clean.

above Inspired by another facet of Southwest history, this dwelling is reminiscent of Old West trading posts. A generous front-porch overhang provides shelter from the sun and inclement weather; front doors open onto a traffic-circle lawn hosting an impressive piece of metal sculpture.

left Peeled-log roof rafters and a handsome plank gate with filigree wrought-iron insets frame the vista of nearby mountains. Their heavy forestation—as well as the foreground leafiness— are testimony to the climatic difference between the mountain Southwest and the lower desert regions.

left This high-elevation garden offers swimming at the top of the world. Situated at the brow of a slope, the pool setting captures an unobstructed, dramatic view of the high plateau and a distant meeting of mountains and sky.

below Milder in summer than the lowlands, and blessed with moisture from rain and snow, the Southwest's high country offers congenial conditions for plants. In this Santa Fe garden, Reiter's creeping thyme, scarlet *Penstemon pinifolius*, and billowy blue oat grass flank a path.

winter gardens

WINTER IS A MAGICAL TIME IN THE HIGH COUNTRY. SNOW DRAPES THE TREES WITH SHAWLS OF WHITE AND DUSTS SEEDHEADS OF DRY GRASSES LIKE POWDERED SUGAR.

In areas like Flagstaff, Taos, and Santa Fe, you can close the door on the garden in winter and turn to indoor pursuits. Or you can take steps to enhance your garden for viewing from indoors. You might call this process snowscaping.

In autumn, refrain from pruning to the ground herbaceous perennials such as Joe Pye weed, statice, and yarrow, or ornamental grasses like *Miscanthus sinensis* 'Purpurascens'. Instead, leave them standing (you can cut them back in late winter). When tufted with snow, these faded mementos of last season's glory have an austere beauty all their own.

For sculptural interest, plant a border of mixed dwarf conifers, such as mugho pine, dwarf Alberta spruce, or a dwarf form of Colorado spruce (*Picea pungens*), where it will define a lawn area or patio. Or flank the front walkway with a cluster of two or three dwarf conifers. Newly fallen snow that flocks the boughs highlights their delicate lines and angles and outlines the shapes of the plants against a backdrop of walls or deciduous trees.

If spots of color are what you're after, paint a garden gate or trellis ice blue or bright coral; it'll make a beautiful accent in a winter white landscape.

this page Given a fine dusting of snow, cactus spines (*above*) somehow appear a bit less fearsome. In the high country, snowfall can make a surprising early appearance, catching blooming plants off guard (*right*). High desert yuccas are silhouetted at sunrise against a blanket of snow (*below*).

facing page Winter transforms the Southwest's high country. Snow on the ground ties everything together like a white lawn; structures and plants are coated with a decorative white frosting that waxes and wanes according to the temperature.

plants

CACTI·SUCCULENTS·LIVING
SCULPTURE·FLOWERING TREES·
SHADE MAKERS·PALMS·CITRUS
·CONIFERS·FLOWERING SHRUBS·
VINES·PERENNIALS·EDIBLES
·WILDFLOWERS·ANNUALS·BULBS·
ROSES·PROBLEM-SOLVER PLANTS

southwest stalwarts

PEOPLE WHO HAVE LIVED IN THE SOUTHWEST for some time often remark that gardening in a water-scarce, heat-dominated region is more an opportunity than a challenge or a hardship. To be sure, many plants common to gardens in moister parts of the country do not perform well here—or fail entirely. Gardeners coming into the area often learn this fact the hard way: all is *not* possible in the Southwest. To appreciate the region's gardening opportunities fully, you need to approach landscaping with your mind open to the possibilities and your eyes open to the plants that succeed in your climate. ◆ The Southwest abounds with natives that thrive here as nowhere else. And these are not merely heroic survivors of nature's adversity— you'll find an abundance and variety of handsome trees, shrubs, perennials, annuals, and signature succulents that make laughable the notion that the Southwest is a Saharan wasteland. Collectively, these well-adapted plants create a distinctive Southwest look that connects the garden to the region's natural landscape and climate.

MENTION THE DESERT SOUTHWEST, AND CACTI AUTOMATICALLY COME
TO MIND. USED NEAR THE GARDEN'S BOUNDARIES, THESE PERFECTLY
ADAPTED PLANTS PROVIDE A LINK TO THE NATIVE VEGETATION.

cacti

A stately saguaro silhouetted in the sunset—what is more
symbolic of the southwestern landscape? Arguably the region's
best-known cactus, the saguaro merely scratches the surface of the
cactus realm. Cacti are the New World flora's exclusive and perfect
response to heat and aridity: plants that store moisture in thickened,
generally tough-skinned bodies, amply protected from thirsty
predators by formidable, spiny armature. In contrast, their silken-
petaled blossoms seem amazingly delicate.

Some familiar cacti are known for their characteristic shapes:
globes, barrels, and columns. Beyond those striking pieces of solid

In a perfect match of landscape to climate, this home garden presents the desert in microcosm.
Featured, among the gravel and boulders, are cacti in their inimitable diversity: a precisely spiny
barrel, a paddle-segmented prickly pear, a bristly cholla, a statuesque cereus, and a stand of
old man cactus looking like an urban skyline in morning sunlight.

geometry are countless others, ranging from sculptural sorts (like the saguaro) to "bushy" plants. Among the bushy types, branches may be cylindrical (like those of the chollas) or flattened (like those of various prickly pears), or have multiple angles in cross section (like those of the organpipe and *Cereus peruvianus*).

Size varies greatly, too. Classic, ancient saguaros top the height range at 50 feet. Established organpipes (*Stenocereus thurberi*) and prickly pears (*Opuntia ficus-indica*) make hefty clumps to 15 feet high and about two-thirds as wide. At the low end is foot-tall beavertail cactus (*Opuntia basilaris*) spreading its prickly pads into broad clumps. The majority of cacti fall between these extremes.

Celebrate these extraordinary plants—even let yourself feel a bit smug—realizing that the Southwest is one of the world's few congenial habitats for them.

The most effective plantings of cacti mimic the plants' natural settings. In the wild, many cacti occur in clumps or grow into small colonies. Even individual plants usually associate closely with desert shrubs or perennials—a lone saguaro, for example, growing from a clump of mesquite.

The majority of cacti grow only in the low and intermediate desert regions (Sunset climate zones 12 and 13) where winters are warm, but a select number of tougher types extend cactus country into chillier areas (zones 10 and 11 and even 2 and 3).

Geometrically symmetrical cactus plants are the perfect Southwest choice for composing a scene of zenlike tranquillity. Here, framed in a bed of gravel, four artfully placed barrel cacti (*Echinocactus grusonii*) are featured in a still-life portrait set before a blank wall perforated by a moon window.

right Desert sunrise illuminates a haze of fine spines on the limbs of this magnificent wild clump of organpipe cactus (*Stenocereus thurberi*); a piece of living architecture, it needs no landscape accompaniment other than this carpet of wildflowers. below A young prickly pear cactus (*Opuntia ficus-indica*) dominates the foreground of this naturalistic sand-and-gravel landscape. In the background are desert wildflowers and drifts of cacti of assorted shapes.

above The natural desert landscape is as colorful as a deliberately designed garden. A look-but-don't-touch teddybear cactus (*Opuntia bigelovii*) makes a silvery statement in front of the mounds of yellow and red shrubs, which contrast in color and shape. left Cactus blossoms are surprisingly silky and showy—as this barrel cactus illustrates in molten lava colors. Behind it, prickly pear pads (*Opuntia ficus-indica*) bear an attractive crop of edible "cactus apples."

Pillars of young saguaros (*Carnegiea gigantea*) are prominent in this garden of desert natives. The treelike palo verde (*Cercidium*) in the background is taller now, but the saguaros will dominate as they gain height and branching.

favorite cacti

FOR WARM-WINTER ZONES (12, 13)

Barrel cactus *Ferocactus* species Globe-shaped young plants mature slowly to cylinders that grow to 9 feet tall; ribs bear clusters of hooked spines.

Old man *Cephalocereus senilis* Slender, slow-growing columns are covered in long, nearly white hairs and yellow spines; can reach 40 feet in great age; needs a bit of shade in zone 13.

Organpipe *Stenocereus thurberi* Hefty, 12-foot-tall clumps consist of columnar, ribbed, green stems; night-blooming flowers produce edible red fruits.

Prickly pear *Opuntia ficus-indica* Plants made of broadly oval, bristly pads may be shrubby or treelike (to 15 feet); flowers on the pad margins form large, roundish, edible fruits—the prickly pears or *nopales* in markets.

Saguaro *Carnegiea gigantea* A monumental, treelike cactus growing at first in a single column for many years, and then slowly developing a few upward-arching branches from the main trunk.

FOR WARM- TO COLDER-WINTER ZONES (10–13)

Barrel cactus *Echinocactus* Stout, cylindrical plants with prominent, spiny ribs; golden barrel, *E. grusonii,* reaches 4 feet high and 2½ feet in diameter.

Christmas cholla *Opuntia leptocaulis* A branching plant typically rising to 3 feet high and wide, with narrow, spiny, cylindrical joints up to 12 inches long; olivelike fruits mature to red in December.

Teddybear cactus *Opuntia bigelovii* A branching, treelike, 3- to 6-foot-tall plant with cylindrical joints covered in silvery spines.

FOR SNOWY-WINTER ZONES (2, 3)

Beavertail cactus *Opuntia basilaris* Thick, oval, long-spined pads can reach 12 inches in length; the branching plant grows little more than 1 foot high but spreads to 4 feet.

Hedgehog cactus *Echinocereus* species Clumps consist of upright, ribbed cylinders; showy flowers and fruits are decorative features.

LIKE CACTI, SUCCULENTS STORE MOISTURE IN THICK, FLESHY LEAVES AND STEMS, ALLOWING THE PLANTS TO SURVIVE PROLONGED STRETCHES OF DRY WEATHER WITH LITTLE OR NO WATERING.

SOUTHWEST STYLE

succulents

Varied and distinctive, succulents come from diverse climates worldwide, but the majority of these plants dislike hot summers and withstand little or no frost. Those that can handle the heat in low-elevation Southwest areas are as welcome in gardens there as the region's native plants.

Among the most useful succulents are several that develop into midsize shrubs. Jade plant (*Crassula ovata*), a pampered houseplant in much of the country, is a dense, billowy, thick-limbed shrub in low and intermediate desert gardens; clusters of starlike pale pink flowers decorate its bright green branches during the cooler months. Similar, but with red-tinted gray-green leaves, is *C. arborescens*. South African elephant's food (*Portulacaria afra*) is cast from the jade plant mold but bears smaller leaves on slimmer stems. Use these plants as specimen shrubs, container plants, or even unclipped hedges.

Other favored succulents include various echeverias —especially those called hen and chicks, which form rosettes—and a number of stonecrops (*Sedum*) from neighboring Mexico. Scatter them as accents in foreground plantings, or grow them in containers to highlight their unusual shapes and colors. Container culture, in fact, offers two distinct advantages: you can move the plants to shadier spots when sun becomes too intense, and you can take them indoors or to other sheltered spots if freezing weather threatens.

above A suspended pot holds a "bouquet" of succulents: two rosette-form echeverias and two sedums— pendant donkey tail and red-tinted pork and beans. far right Late summer flowers of *Sedum telephium* are a favorite in cold-winter gardens. right Massed hen and chicks (*Echeveria*) create a portrait in precise geometric forms.

IN NATURE'S GALLERY, THE TRADEMARK NATIVE CACTI OF THE SOUTHWEST KEEP COMPANY WITH AN ARRAY OF UNRELATED BUT EQUALLY STRIKING SCULPTURAL PLANTS.

living sculpture

Like cacti, many living sculpture plants hail from the Southwest and are perfectly attuned to the climatic rigors of the region. Some even bear protective spines, or at least spine-tipped leaves. But in all other ways, these plants stake out their own individuality.

Various agaves and aloes feature straplike leaves arranged in striking rosettes. Agave leaves are broad, fleshy, and tough, often with spines on the edges or tips. Use their varied colors—from green to silvery blue-gray to cream-and-gray combinations—to accent a contrasting area of your garden. The 10-foot-wide century plant (*Agave americana*) is the giant of the group; 1-foot-wide *A. victoriae-reginae* is positively petite by comparison. Agaves don't bloom annually, but, when they do, striking flowers appear on tall stems rising well above the mass of leaves.

Aloes, too, have fleshy leaves in green to gray-green shades, often mottled with contrasting colors. Some have spiny edges, but they are not as ferocious as

left Young Mexican blue palms (*Brahea armata*) stand in stark relief against a white stucco wall, perfectly reflected in a still pool. These plants grow slowly to 20 to 40 feet; on mature palms, showy cream-colored flowers appear in long, pendant streamers.

Feature palms for their dramatic, distinctive forms. Situate a clump-forming palm where it will be a natural focal point, with other plantings subordinate. Single-trunk palms are especially striking when placed where their majesty is reflected in a pool of still water. In larger gardens, plant a row of them to create a living colonnade. All palms make stunning nighttime statements when lights at their base are trained upward to illuminate the trunks and fronds.

above Stately queen palms (*Syagrus romanzoffianum*) splay their elegant, featherlike fronds above a Spanish-style, tile-roofed home. At the trunk bases is a cluster of pygmy date palms (*Phoenix roebelenii*), a diminutive relative of the towering commercial date producer.
left The swimming pool serves as an elegant mirror for a stand of mature Mexican fan palms.

Although most palms require the mild-winter temperatures of zones 12 and 13, these four extend palm territory into colder regions: California fan palm (*Washingtonia filifera*), zones 10 (warmer parts), 11–13; Mediterranean fan palm (*Chamaerops humilis*), zones 10, 11; Mexican blue palm (*Brahea armata*), zones 10, 12, 13; and Mexican fan palm (*Washingtonia robusta*), zones 10 (warmer parts), 11–13.

IN INTERMEDIATE AND LOW DESERT CLIMATES, YOU HAVE THE ENVIABLE
OPPORTUNITY TO GROW ANY KIND OF CITRUS FRUIT YOU WANT.

citrus

Orange, lemon, lime, grapefruit, mandarin, kumquat, and more—
choose your favorite and plant it. You'll have enough heat to ripen the
fruit properly, and you won't have a serious freeze that could destroy
the plant. If you choose varieties care-
fully, you can have citrus fruit of some
kind available for eating any time of
year. And various types of citrus offer
that best of combinations: edible crops
from distinguished garden plants.
Glossy leaves make a dense foliage
cover that looks good throughout the
year; wonderfully fragrant blossoms
perfume the air in season; and the
orange or yellow fruits are strikingly
decorative.

All citrus plants tend to look like
oversize shrubs, but inherent plant size
varies. The largest, tallest plants (and
the ones most likely to become treelike)
are the grapefruits—rising to about
25 feet at maturity. Next in line are
oranges and some lemons, growing to
around 20 feet. They are followed by
'Meyer' lemon, limes, mandarins, and
tangelos, which reach about 15 feet.
Kumquats may attain 15 feet, but
heights of 6 to 10 feet are more common. To add to your choices, many

From Moorish Spain to the New World
came the practice of growing citrus trees
in large terra-cotta pots. This navel orange
on dwarfing rootstock bears consistently,
yet never outgrows the container; the stucco
wall and gravel footing ensure enough
heat for best-quality fruit.

popular varieties of all types are available grafted onto dwarfing rootstock, which reduces the ultimate size; these are good candidates for planting in large containers. And if you want several kinds in limited space, some nurseries offer "cocktail citrus," which have different types of citrus grafted onto a single rootstock.

Versatility is a citrus trademark. All kinds make handsome shrubs of various sizes, useful for background and intermediate positions in your garden. The larger plants can be trimmed up to become moderate-size trees; the smaller to midsize kinds, planted 4 to 6 feet apart in rows, can be maintained as fruiting hedges. And citrus are classic plants for growing in large containers.

top A broad, shallow container offers enough root room for this dwarf mandarin ("tangerine"). above Decorative kumquat fruits grace shrubs that are handsome all year. left Tight quarters are no problem for citrus. A narrow raised bed hosts a thriving lemon, pruned to spread out against the wall behind.

SOUTHWEST GARDENS ARE HOME TO A RANGE OF EVERGREEN CONIFERS, FROM TALL, STATELY PINES TO LARGE, SHRUBBY TYPES THAT CAN PROVIDE SHELTER FROM WIND OR SCREENS FOR PRIVACY.

conifers

You may think pines and their cone-bearing allies belong in rugged mountain terrain, and, indeed, they are prominent trees in the Southwest's mountainous territory. But a number of them also are at home—even as natives—in lower-elevation desert regions.

Among the loosely related trees and shrubs whose leaves are needles or scales, you'll find considerable variation in shapes and foliage colors. Italian stone pine (*Pinus pinea*) matures to a distinctive broad tabletop silhouette, its massive framework softened by a dense canopy of dark green needles. Aleppo pine (*P. halepensis*), in contrast, carries its light green needles on an irregularly upright, open structure. Calabrian pine (*P. brutia*) and Afghan pine (*P. eldarica*) are more symmetrical versions of Aleppo pine with darker needles. All three tolerate poor soil, drought, and wind.

Bright green, scalelike foliage in flattened sprays immediately sets apart incense cedar (*Calocedrus decurrens*), as does its symmetrical, cone-shaped outline. A large, pyramid-shaped shrub, scale-leafed Arizona cypress (*Cupressus arizonica*) comes in a range of colors: green to blue-gray to nearly silver.

The larger conifers make splendidly picturesque accent trees, and some of them also perform valuable duty as windbreaks. Use the shrubby piñon pines (*P. edulis, P. cembroides, P. monophylla*) and Arizona cypress in the landscape as background plantings, providing unchanging foils for more colorful garden associates.

NOTE: Recent episodes of prolonged drought have hit pines hard, even native species. Drought-stressed trees attract bark beetles, which invade, then kill, their hosts. Some experts even suggest that you avoid planting piñon pines. If you must plant a pine, be prepared to water it in drought years— a deep soaking (roughly 3 inches of water per month) during the normal rainfall period.

choice conifers

FOR HIGH-ELEVATION ZONES (2, 3, 10)

Coulter pine *Pinus coulteri*
Incense cedar *Calocedrus decurrens*
Mexican piñon pine *Pinus cembroides*
Piñon *Pinus edulis*
Singleleaf piñon pine *Pinus monophylla*

FOR LOWER-ELEVATION ZONES (11–13)

Afghan pine *Pinus eldarica*
Aleppo pine *Pinus halepensis*
Arizona cypress *Cupressus arizonica*
Mexican piñon pine *Pinus cembroides*

FOR WARM-WINTER ZONES (12, 13)

Calabrian pine *Pinus brutia*
Canary Island pine *Pinus canariensis*
Chir pine *Pinus roxburghii*
Italian stone pine *Pinus pinea*

facing page Loggers know it as one of the West's premier timber trees, but ponderosa pine (*Pinus ponderosa*) also adapts well to life in Southwest gardens, where it adds a touch of mountain atmosphere. Growing symmetrically upright fairly rapidly, ponderosas can ultimately reach heights of 100 feet. above One of the Southwest's stellar native plants, Arizona cypress (*Cupressus arizonica*) thrives in gardens from high desert to low. It shines as a symmetrical accent (ultimately reaching 40 feet), and the dense growth makes it a fine windbreak plant. right Unlike the sky-piercing pine trees of mountainous regions, Southwest native piñon (*Pinus edulis*) becomes an ever-larger shrub as it matures. Its cones are a source of edible seeds sold as pine nuts.

TO REAP RELIABLE GARDEN COLOR WITH THE LEAST AMOUNT OF GARDENING EFFORT, YOU CAN'T FIND A BETTER CHOICE THAN FLOWERING SHRUBS.

flowering shrubs

Year after year shrubs deliver their floral bounty, asking only a modicum of care: a bit of water (less or more, depending on the shrub) and the occasional pruning. Color is just one of their features. All these plants contribute mass and bulk to a garden area, serving as a permanent framework—or permanent focal points—largely unchanged from one year to the next. At your disposal are shrubs from tall to short, skinny to spreading, dense to filmy, with a seemingly endless array of foliage shapes and textures to complement an equally diverse assortment of flower sizes, shapes, and colors.

Gardeners in the Southwest can enjoy many flowering shrubs widely grown in other parts of the country. But their special privilege is to grow an exciting assortment of shrubs native to the territory and from other low-rainfall regions of the world. Desert honeysuckle, Apache plume, feather bush, fairy duster, Texas mountain laurel—these evocative names are just a sampling of Southwest specialty shrubs well worth cultivating. If you pay attention to individual flowering periods, you can choose a shrub assortment that will give you color in all four seasons.

top Shrubs provide a garden's backbone, and the best offer beauty as well. The foreground English lavender (*Lavandula angustifolia*) is successful from the mountains to the low desert. Its soft lilac wands are a soothing contrast to the vivid red-and-yellow flowers of perennial rudbeckia.

right In summer and fall, autumn sage (*Salvia greggii*) delivers a nonstop flower show on bushy, rounded plants growing to 4 feet tall. Flame red is a typical color, but flowers also come in red-purple, pinks, and white.
below Tropical native *Caesalpinia pulcherrima* is known by several common names, including pride of Barbados and dwarf poinciana. Reaching 10 feet tall and wide, it enlivens intermediate and low desert gardens with flamboyant flowers and feathery leaves throughout the warm season.

below A luxuriant Texas ranger (*Leucophyllum frutescens*) plant produces clustered blossoms in bursts throughout the year; purple is the usual color, but pink- and white-flowered kinds are available. The plant's soft, lush appearance belies a tough, drought-tolerant constitution— as this pairing with native ocotillo (on the left) demonstrates.

above The bright red blossoms of Baja fairy duster (*Calliandra californica*) are beloved both because of their delicacy and because they are irresistible to hummingbirds.

right In the heat of summer a splash of refreshing blue is always welcome. That's what you get from chaste tree (*Vitex agnus-castus*), which continues its show of fragrant blossoms well into fall.

above For brightness, choose Mexican honeysuckle (*Justicia spicigera,* sometimes sold as *Anisacanthus thurberi*); blooms peak in spring and fall but appear all year on this 3-foot-high, spreading plant. Here, Southwest native perennial scarlet hedge nettle (*Stachys coccinea*) adds to the brilliance. right Perfectly at home either in containers or in the ground, shrimp plant (*Justicia brandegeeana*) reliably offers its small white blossoms in distinctive, shrimplike spikes for a long stretch from spring through fall in lower-elevation desert gardens.

native shrubs

Apache plume *Fallugia paradoxa*

Autumn sage *Salvia greggii*

Baja fairy duster *Calliandra californica*

Black dalea *Dalea frutescens*

Brittlebush *Encelia farinosa*

Chuparosa *Justicia californica*

Desert honeysuckle *Anisacanthus thurberi*

Desert sage *Salvia dorrii*

Fairy duster *Calliandra eriophylla*

Feather bush *Lysiloma thornberi*

Indigo bush *Dalea bicolor* and *D. pulchra*

Jamé sage *Salvia × jamensis*

Mexican bird of paradise *Calliandra mexicana*

Mexican honeysuckle *Justicia spicigera*

Ruellia californica

Senna wislizenii

Shrimp plant *Justicia brandegeeana*

Texas mountain laurel *Sophora secundiflora*

Texas ranger *Leucophyllum frutescens*

above Yellow bells (*Tecoma stans*) brings a touch of the tropics from late spring to early winter in mild-winter Southwest gardens. Where frost is absent, these plants can attain tree stature. top right A sentimental favorite in cold-winter climates, common lilac (*Syringa vulgaris*) also thrives in all but the lower-elevation zones of the Southwest. Every spring, these bulky plants present a lavish pageant of famously fragrant flowers in shades of lavender, purple, pink, and white. right Wisteria-like blossoms adorn bulky plants of Texas mountain laurel (*Sophora secundiflora*) from midwinter to early spring.

THINK OF VINES AS COLORFUL DRAPERY FOR THE GARDEN. THESE LIMBER PLANTS OFFER
A RELAXED EASINESS, LOOKING AS THOUGH THE PULL OF GRAVITY MIGHT WIN.

vines

You might plant vines to make shade from an overhead arbor, to smother a
fence, or to form an intricate foliage tracery on a trellis or pillar. They aren't
essential to a garden, but often they provide just the right finishing touch.

Mexico and South America are home to the bulk of the Southwest's best vines—
plants able to flourish in the summer heat without flinching. Some of the most
colorful of these are at peak bloom during the hottest months: coral vine (*Antigonon
leptopus*), bougainvillea, violet trumpet vine (*Clytostoma callistegioides*), and orchid
vine (*Mascagnia* species) are good examples. In low desert gardens, you can enjoy
lavish color in winter from flame vine (*Pyrostegia venusta*) and Cape honeysuckle
(*Tecoma capensis*), while Lady Banks' rose (*Rosa banksiae* 'Lutea') straddles the line
between winter and spring.

In using vines for structural adornment, you have the chance to play with colors
as well as textures. Solid adobe walls, for example, are wonderful foils for
bougainvilleas in brilliant orange or vibrant purple. Wooden structures weathered
to shades of gray and silver are enhanced by floral displays of white and all shades
of pink. A white background pleasantly sets off lavender, blue, and soft yellow
blossoms, while it makes the most stark contrast possible to red.

above In high-altitude areas (zones 1–3), summer is mild enough to encourage stellar performance
from Jackman clematis (*Clematis × jackmanii*), a vigorous, fast-growing vine that adds a cool dash
of purple to this planting of summer flowers in hot colors.

right In an ample container, nectar-rich perennials attract hummingbirds. The wispy spikes of bright red are *Penstemon* × *gloxinioides* 'Firebird'; the darkest red flowers belong to *Salvia greggii*; purple is furnished by Mexican sage (*Salvia leucantha,* at the top) and *Salvia guaranitica*; and Cape fuchsia (*Phygelius capensis* 'Scarlet') provides the pendant blossoms in coral-red.

above A showy clump of perennial 'Moonshine' yarrow (*Achillea*) thrives in high-altitude southwestern zones. A daylily (*Hemerocallis*) in complementary warm colors peeks from behind it on the left, while on the right stands a blood-red dahlia, a favorite bulb of the region. right Blue catmint (*Nepeta* × *faassenii*) is the theme plant of this high-altitude perennial garden. Drifts of it are interrupted by a patch of rosy red Jupiter's beard (*Centranthus ruber*). Masses of yellow-flowered columbine light up the background.

left Old-fashioned hollyhocks (*Alcea rosea*) come in a wide color range; although naturally biennials, they can be short-lived perennials where summers are mild. below A riotous mix of perennials swamps a New Mexico garden. Rosy violet phlox (*Phlox paniculata*) dominates the foreground, accompanied by red bee balm (*Monarda didyma*) and a creamy daylily; farther back, hollyhock spires rise above assorted yellow daisies (*Rudbeckia*).

far left The Southwest's own native sunflower, *Helianthus maximilianii*, hoists its golden bounty on stems rising to 10 feet. Easy to grow, it thrives in all the region's climate zones. left Rich blue Rocky Mountain penstemon (*Penstemon strictus*), another native, is suited to both high- and low-altitude gardens. Early summer flowers come on stems to 3 feet high. Rosy Jupiter's beard (*Centranthus ruber*) and yellow sunrose (*Helianthemum nummularium*) provide background color contrast.

right Native chocolate flower (*Berlandiera lyrata*) is worth growing for its delicious fragrance alone, which can perfume the surroundings in spring and summer. below Long-blooming Mexican hat (*Ratibida columnifera*) flaunts its festive blossoms on 2½-foot stems from summer into fall.

below Foolproof purple coneflower (*Echinacea purpurea*) is a perennial standby in much of the Southwest. Stems 2 to 4 feet tall carry rosy purple or white daisies with yellow, orange, or purple centers. At higher altitudes, it blooms in summer and into fall; in low and intermediate desert gardens, flowers start in spring before summer heat strikes.

native perennials

Beard tongue *Penstemon* species

Blackfoot daisy *Melampodium leucanthum*

California fuchsia *Zauschneria californica latifolia*

Chocolate flower *Berlandiera lyrata*

Coahuila sage *Salvia coahuilensis*

Copper Canyon daisy *Tagetes lemmonii*

Evening primrose *Oenothera* species

Gaura *Gaura lindheimeri*

Globe mallow *Sphaeralcea* species

Helianthus maximilianii

Mexican hat *Ratibida columnifera*

Paper daisy *Psilostrophe cooperi*

Sundrops *Calylophus* species

CORN, SQUASH, CHILI PEPPERS—WELL BEFORE THE ARRIVAL OF EUROPEAN SETTLERS, SOUTHWEST NATIVE AMERICAN AGRICULTURE CENTERED ON THESE AND OTHER KEY CROPS.

edibles

Today native edibles are an integral part of southwestern culture. Mingling them with exotic edibles and herbs brought to the area through initial Spanish contact creates a rich mixture of two traditions. In the Southwest, gardens and edibles are intertwined as nowhere else in the country.

Many traditional vegetables, fruits, and herbs are ornamental assets to a garden. Peppers, tomatoes, and tomatillos give you full, leafy plants with decorative fruits. Squash plants offer dramatic foliage and colorful blossoms. Beans provide leafy cover wherever you might use an annual vine, while a hill of corn plants is as compelling as any ornamental grass. For drama, look to a large, seed-bearing sunflower.

To enjoy success with these traditional plants, choose varieties that suit your particular region (see "Chiles, Not Chilis," facing page). Oftentimes you'll find that the methods used by original inhabitants still are the best.

above left Purple corn (*Zea mays*) is a colorful variant of the familiar edible *maize* crop long cultivated by the Southwest's native inhabitants. below A season's bounty of winter squashes, another staple crop cultivated by native peoples of the region since prehistoric times, spills out of a rustic cart.

CHILES, NOT CHILIS

Responding to a magazine article about "chili," one New Mexican couple wrote, "We don't eat chili in New Mexico. We eat chile." The first spelling is standard English, while the second is Spanish and southwestern English.

Does it matter? "You bet," says Dr. Paul Bosland, who heads chile research at New Mexico State University in Las Cruces. "New Mexico even has an official state question: red or green?"

Chiles are Southwest originals, harvested in the wild (as *chiltepíns*) for millennia. When Spaniards started settling the region in the 16th century, they brought improved chile varieties up from Mexico. Many of those early chiles—ones like Chimayo, Vilarde, and Española—are still grown.

Fresh, the chile is a vegetable; dried, it's a spice. "People forget that Columbus came to the New World in search of spices," says Bosland. "They were more precious than gold, so he took tomato and chile seeds back to Spain with him." Everybody loved these hot, bright fruits, and chiles spread quickly around the world. By the time a French taxonomist classified them, they were so deeply embedded in Asian cuisine that he assumed they must be Chinese, and he called a major South American chile species *Capsicum chinense*. The name still stands.

Though New Mexico is the epicenter of the chile world, the passion for chiles is global. Bosland started the research-based Chile Pepper Institute (www.chilepepperinstitute.org) a few years ago when requests for information about chiles made it hard for him to focus on chile research. Now a staffer and graduate students handle the queries, the trial gardens, and the list of members, who span 50 states and 36 countries.

Chiles offer more than flavor: they also make you feel good. "When a chile pepper burns your mouth," says Bosland, "your body makes endorphins to counter the pain. Those endorphins are mood elevators, but they're not addictive. How much of a lift do they give? About what you'd get from a cup of coffee."

If you want to grow chiles, start with a selection that runs from sweet to very hot. Bosland suggests you plant some Jalapeños (green, maturing to red), a few 'NuMex Joe E. Parker' peppers for a New Mexico pod type (green, ripening to red; 'Anaheim' is the best-known of these), and some fiery hot 'Red Savina' Habaneros (small, pointed, green, maturing to red). For fullest flavor, let them color completely before harvest. String together a *ristra* of 'NuMex Joe E. Parker' peppers for drying on the south side of your house. By season's end, you'll have a garden full of red, green, orange, and yellow chiles. And when somebody asks "What color?" just say "Christmas."

SOUTHWEST STYLE

wildflowers

"SEE THE DESERT IN BLOOM" PROCLAIMED THE EARLY 20TH-CENTURY SALES PITCH TO LURE TRAVELERS TO THE SOUTHWEST, WHERE CARPETS OF FLOWERS IN THE ARID LANDSCAPE ASTONISHED VISITORS.

While a wildflower show is not a yearly phenomenon in nature—timely rainfall is the key—you can guarantee one in your garden as long as you control the growing conditions.

You don't need a large expanse of ground for a wildflower display. These plants work just as well in small "pocket" plantings or popping up as seasonal color among beds of cacti, agaves, and other desert plants.

Seed them initially into prepared soil in fall, and both annual and perennial wildflowers will reappear year after year by natural reseeding—although what predominates one year may not be the most abundant flower the next. That's the beauty of wildflower gardening: you capture the spontaneity of nature.

reliable wild annuals and perennials

YELLOW

Bahia *Bahia absinthifolia*

Bigelow's coreopsis *Coreopsis bigelovii*

Chinchweed *Pectis papposa*

Coastal tidytips *Layia platyglossa*

Cooper's paperflower *Psilostrophe cooperi*

Desert marigold *Baileya multiradiata*

Dyssodia *Dyssodia pentachaeta*

Goldfields *Baeria chrysostoma*

Mexican tulip poppy *Hunnemannia fumariifolia*

Yellowblanket *Lesquerella gordonii*

ORANGE

Apricot mallow *Sphaeralcea ambigua*

California poppy *Eschscholzia californica*

Mexican gold poppy *Eschscholzia mexicana*

RED

Firecracker penstemon *Penstemon eatonii*

Firewheel *Gaillardia pulchella*

PINK

Canyon penstemon *Penstemon pseudospectabilis*

Owl's clover *Orthocarpus purpurascens*

Parry's penstemon *Penstemon parryi*

BLUE AND LAVENDER

Arizona lupine *Lupinus arizonicus*

Arroyo lupine *Lupinus succulentus*

Bigelow's aster *Machaeranthera bigelovii*

Chia *Salvia columbariae*

Coulter's lupine *Lupinus sparsiflorus*

Desert bluebell *Phacelia campanularia*

Fleabane *Erigeron divergens*

Goodding's verbena *Verbena gooddingii*

Wild delphinium *Delphinium scaposum*

WHITE

Birdcage evening primrose *Oenothera deltoides*

Blackfoot daisy *Melampodium leucanthum*

Desert chicory *Rafinesquia neomexicana*

Fragrant evening primrose *Oenothera caespitosa*

facing page This domesticated desert features only native wildflowers. Foreground color consists of orange California poppy, white fragrant evening primrose, gray-leafed desert marigold, and vivid desert bluebells. Across the path, more desert marigolds are joined by yellow brittlebush and pink penstemon. facing page inset Desert bluebell (*Phacelia campanularia*). above Architectural accent colors are cleverly repeated in this springtime wildflower meadow. Scarlet flax (*Linum perenne* 'Rubrum') dominates the foreground, scattered through drifts of blue lupine and taller wands of pink penstemon.

FOR BRINGING MASS COLOR TO THE GARDEN, NOTHING WORKS BETTER
THAN ANNUALS. GARDENERS AVIDLY PLANT THESE BOUNTIFUL PLANTS FOR
IN-A-HURRY EFFECTS.

annuals

Though annuals are gone in a year, they typically give you flowers throughout most of their lives. The phrase "flower factory" perfectly describes them.

Annuals fall into two broad categories: cool-season (blooming in winter and spring) and warm-season (blooming in summer). What you choose and when you plant depend on where you live in the Southwest. If you're in an intermediate or low desert region (zones 12 and 13), where summer temperatures are incandescent and winters usually cool to mild, you can plant cool-season annuals from October to mid-November to reap flowers beginning in winter and continuing into spring until hot weather shuts them down. Plant your warm-season annuals in late winter and early spring, and choose varieties that prefer summer heat; treat the heat-intolerant types as if they were cool-season plants.

For gardens in the high and medium desert zones (10 and 11), your growing window for cool-season annuals is a fairly short period between winter frosts and spring heat. Plant in late winter to early spring (when frosts have become light). You can set out warm-season annuals in midspring.

Prolific cosmos (*Cosmos bipinnatus*) delivers color reliably in all Southwest climate zones. Vigorous old-fashioned plants reach head height, but newer strains grow only 2 to 4 feet. Color runs from white and pink to magenta and purple—including fetching bicolor combinations.

best annuals

COOL-SEASON

Calendula *Calendula officinalis*
Iceland poppy *Papaver nudicaule*
Larkspur *Consolida ajacis*
Pansy *Viola × wittrockiana*
Snapdragon *Antirrhinum majus*

WARM-SEASON

Annual coreopsis *Coreopsis tinctoria*
Annual sunflower *Helianthus annuus*
Cockscomb *Celosia*
Cosmos *Cosmos bipinnatus*
Garden verbena *Verbena × hybrida*
Globe amaranth *Gomphrena globosa*
*Impatiens *Impatiens walleriana*
*Lobelia *Lobelia erinus*
Madagascar periwinkle
   Catharanthus roseus
Marigold *Tagetes* species
Mexican sunflower *Tithonia rotundifolia*
*Petunia *Petunia × hybrida*
Rose moss *Portulaca grandiflora*
Scarlet sage *Salvia splendens*
Zinnia *Zinnia* species

*Heat-intolerant. Plant with cool-season
 annuals if you live in low desert areas.

In the high-altitude zones (1–3), winters are both cold
and long. Spring moves quickly into summer weather—
which ranges from fairly hot to fairly mild, as the altitude
increases. In these gardens, plant the fast-maturing warm-
season annuals after the normal last-frost date. If you live
in the cooler of these zones (1 and 2), cool-season annuals
planted in the fall may perform tirelessly throughout
the summer.

above This vivid planting fairly shouts "Fiesta!" Annual zinnias (*Zinnia elegans*)
dominate the foreground, while orange and yellow French marigolds
(*Tagetes patula*) border the pathway at left. The annuals complement the
colors of the thriving clump of cannas, a foolproof summer-flowering bulb.
top right Impressive blooms of the common sunflower (*Helianthus annuus*).

THE SHOWY FLOWERS OF BULBS FIT BEAUTIFULLY INTO THE SOUTHWEST GARDEN,
BRINGING COLOR YEAR AFTER YEAR JUST WHERE YOU WANT A SPLASH OF BRIGHTNESS.

bulbs

Bulbs are plants that store energy in a part of their anatomy below the ground, so that they can repeat their performance of leaves and flowers the following year. The broad category includes not only true bulbs but also corms, tubers, rhizomes, and tuberous roots.

In the lower-elevation, mild-winter southwestern zones (12, 13, 18–20), you can have various bulbs in flower from winter into fall. In the colder-winter zones (1–3, 10, 11), the bulbs that bloom earliest start flowering at the beginning of spring, while some summer-blooming kinds last until frost. In all parts of the Southwest, bulbs are favorite container plants, valued for lavish seasonal color.

When choosing bulbs, consider three factors: how cold your winters may become, how intense your summer heat is, and how much water you have. In milder-winter zones you can successfully grow the more tender bulbs, such as freesias, and those that flower early and go dormant over summer, such as daffodils. Some mild-winter gardeners do grow traditional cold-winter favorites (hyacinths and tulips, for example), but they chill the bulbs before planting them, choose beds in light shade, and consider the bulbs annuals.

If you live in a region where subfreezing winter temperatures are the norm, you can't leave the more tender bulbs in the ground over winter, but cold-loving varieties like tulips may thrive. In the higher-altitude regions with shorter summers, you can choose summer-blooming bulbs, provided your temperatures aren't extreme.

With wild antecedents native to Mexico, dahlias have a special place in Southwest gardens. Flowers come in a wide range of colors, sizes, and styles; plants range from foot-high bedding types to shrubby 6- to 8-foot giants like this fiery 'Orange Julius'.

above This lush planting of lippia (*Phyla nodiflora*) in low desert Arizona makes a green oasis with none of the fussing and watering required by a lawn. Fountains of Mexican grass tree (*Nolina longifolia*) punctuate the carpet of green.

above Lemon bottlebrush offers more than just dense screening: in low and intermediate desert gardens, clusters of flaming red flowers appear in bursts throughout the year. The shrub can reach 15 feet high, but lower-growing selections are sold. left Prostrate, wide-spreading bearberry cotoneaster (*Cotoneaster dammeri*) thrives in all Southwest climate zones. White blossoms in spring become pea-size red fruits in fall and winter.

best problem solvers

WINDBREAKS

Aleppo pine *Pinus halepensis*
*Arizona cypress *Cupressus arizonica*
Beefwood *Casuarina* species
*Cajeput tree *Melaleuca quinquenervia*
Honey mesquite *Prosopis glandulosa*
*Incense cedar *Calocedrus decurrens*
Osage orange *Maclura pomifera*
*Russian olive *Elaeagnus angustifolia*

*Also good screening plants.

SHRUBS FOR SCREENING

Common buckthorn *Rhamnus cathartica*
Hop bush *Dodonaea viscosa*
Lemon bottlebrush *Callistemon citrinus*
Myrtle *Myrtus communis*
Oleander *Nerium oleander*
Pineapple guava *Feijoa sellowiana*
Texas ranger *Leucophyllum frutescens*
Xylosma congestum

GROUND COVER PERENNIALS

Aptenia cordifolia and *A. c.* 'Red Apple'
Gazania *Gazania* hybrids
Gazania *Gazania linearis* 'Colorado Gold'
Mexican evening primrose *Oenothera speciosa*
Santa Barbara daisy *Erigeron karvinskianus*
Trailing African daisy *Osteospermum fruticosum*
Verbena *Verbena* (many types)

GROUND COVER SHRUBS

Aaron's beard *Hypericum calycinum*
Acacia redolens 'Desert Carpet'
Australian saltbush *Atriplex semibaccata*
Bearberry cotoneaster *Cotoneaster dammeri*
Dwarf coyote brush *Baccharis pilularis*
  (ground cover selections)
Trailing indigo bush *Dalea greggii*
Trailing lantana *Lantana montevidensis*

design

GARDEN ART·CONTAINERS·FIREPITS
·FURNITURE·GATES·WALLS·LIGHTS·
PAINT·PAVING·SHADE STRUCTURES
·WATER FEATURES·WINTER ACCENTS

born of the region

A GARDEN IS LIKE A STAGE. You can keep it simple and predictable, with a lawn, patio, and trees. Or let your imagination soar and design it with theatrical panache, using paint colors, fabric, statuary, and sculptural containers to create bold effects. Either way, good garden design starts with hardscape—the paving, firepits, water features, or seat walls that fit the style of your house. Beyond that, decorative objects you bring in as finishing touches give your garden personality and charm. Whether you paint a bench in the colors and motifs of a Navajo blanket or set a bright red coyote of carved wood in a patch of yellow desert marigolds, you are expressing your passions or playfulness, or your connection to the land and culture that surround you.

LIKE ICING ON A CAKE, ART DECORATES AND ENHANCES THE GARDEN AND
CAN TRANSFORM IT FROM ORDINARY TO MAGICAL.

garden art

In the Southwest, decorative objects born of the culture—such as brightly painted folk art animals and figurines made of Mexican terra-cotta—make beautiful garden accents. But outdoor art can be anything you want it to be: a wooden bench painted in bright primary colors, *ristras* of glossy, bright red chiles dangling from a post beside a garden gate, a stone metate (ancient Indian mortar and pestle), or a couple of round, cream-colored clay pots leaning against an adobe wall. Even a *horno* (the igloo-shaped adobe oven of the region) becomes a work of art against a backdrop of wildflowers and grasses.

When you select large pieces of art, make sure they harmonize with the style of your house, and place them so that they don't overwhelm a small landscape. Tuck smaller pieces as surprises among greenery or at turns in a path; space them well apart to avoid a cluttered look.

A brightly painted folk-art señorita offers a bountiful Southwest harvest: squashes, squash blossoms, and gourds—all staples in Native American culture. Continuing the theme is the backdrop of native sunflower, *Helianthus maximilianii*.

above Decorated in native American symbols, this life-size red steed gazes at garden visitors. Behind it, the house wall and even the cosmos blossoms display colors that complement, but don't overshadow, the animal's scarlet "coat." right Brilliant poppies casually swarming around a craggy tree trunk make a lovely garden picture. But add a piece of artwork, and the scene really comes alive. Here, the art is nothing more than an old bedpost, imaginatively painted and decorated.

How cool can you get? In this carefully planned composition, glacial tints prevail, from ice blue through silver to nearly white. The colors and overall shape of the foreground century plant (*Agave americana*) are repeated, in stylized form, by the sculpturally precise pyramid just behind it. Softening the spiky sharpness is the background drift of bush germander (*Teucrium fruticans*).

right One person's junk is another's art. Here, an industrial-strength bull with headlight eyes fairly radiates personality. Framing it, and creating pattern on the blue concrete wall, are two sets of mattress springs. On the ground, a collection of objets d'art rests among agaves and grasses.

above A humorous tromp l'oeil of a "caged" chicken forms the centerpiece of this composition beneath a strand of dried chiles. Garlic also accompanies the bird—perhaps another ingredient in a main-course recipe? right A classic urn-as-fountain is nothing unusual—even one, like this, with a lovely raku glaze. But add a group of oversize metal bees poised at the top and—voilà!—you have a unique piece of garden art. The color of the blue bees is repeated in a Southwest standard: tiles to line a pool.

right Making a dramatic appearance in a landscape of native plants that blends into the wide open desert beyond, this Southwest folk-art red pony appears to paw the ground as though impatient for a gallop off to the distant mountains.

left Artistic elements here represent three facets of the region's culture. Clay water jugs on pedestals stem from Native American tradition; the statue of a mission padre reflects Spanish influence; and the wagon wheel symbolizes settlers who came overland from the east. below Practical ceramic pieces made by the native inhabitants now have the status of fine art. Typical are this utilitarian shallow bowl and decorated water jar.

left This massive wall niche houses religious icons from Mexican tradition brought to the Southwest by Spanish missionaries. While the symbolism is from the Old World, the artistic renditions show clear imprints of New World cultures.

above Viva Mexico! From the heavy timbers and thick, plastered walls to the brightly colored artistic details, everything here is an homage to south of the border. Piñatas dangling from roof beams hover above riotous flowering plants—crocosmia, Dahlberg daisies, New Guinea impatiens, nicotiana, zinnias—springing from decorated pottery; terra-cotta balls and melon slices contribute artistic humor.

left In contrast, this garden vignette is a strictly Southwestern portrait. Native sunflowers (*Helianthus maximilianii*) crowd in on drying bunches of the region's characteristic red chile peppers suspended from a twiggy fence.

IN TODAY'S GARDENS, PLANT CONTAINERS ARE BEAUTIFUL AND UNUSUAL ART FORMS YOU CAN USE TO ADD DRAMA TO YOUR OUTDOOR DECOR.

containers

In their myriad shapes, colors, sizes, and compositions, today's containers are as versatile as they are portable. Sometimes they function as complements to the plants they hold; sometimes they are the dominant features, while the plants take a secondary role; and some containers are strategically placed as sculptural pieces bearing no plants at all.

Southwest tradition, combining Native American and Spanish elements, emphasizes earthenware vessels. These clay containers—either decorated in Native American motifs or unadorned but textured (reflecting Spanish influence)—harmonize well with any garden hardscape that features natural and traditional materials. In outdoor settings of less traditional style, terra-cotta containers serve as accents that highlight the region's cultural roots. But containers need not reflect regional heritage. Some of the most effective ones simply take their color and design cues from the surrounding desert.

To better cope with the region's heat and dryness, choose less-thirsty plants for container culture, and group containers so they give a bit of shade to one another.

Traditional terra-cotta, the perfect complement to Southwest adobe, gains new elegance in these simple, clean-lined pots. Their architectural angularity perfectly displays a collection of sculptural plants: nolina (*top left*), agave (*top right*), and echeveria (*foreground*).

above This terra-cotta pot hosts a lively array of annuals—to the apparent bemusement of a Southwest folk-art carved horse. above right Arrayed as though they were in a sculpture gallery, simple clay containers at the rear display native cacti, while a terra-cotta cylinder in the foreground shows off an exuberant bouquet of blossoming acacia stems. right A beautiful grayed ceramic *olla* (water jar) lounges as sculpture in a wall corner, surrounded by plants in the ground rather than bursting with plants inside it. below Colored containers complete this veritable rhapsody in blue. The featured grayish-blue aloe is the container centerpiece, surrounded by a row of petite aloes in a slightly darker hue.

A wall-mounted wire basket lined with moss holds drought-tolerant succulent sedums and echeverias; prominent in the foreground is a "waterfall" of donkey tail sedum (*Sedum morganianum*).

WHEN BALMY AFTERNOONS GIVE WAY TO CHILLY DESERT EVENINGS, A TOASTY FIRE MAKES THE GARDEN OR PATIO THE PERFECT PLACE TO GATHER.

firepits

After sundown, flickering firelight enhances courtyards and creates a feeling of intimacy outdoors. Most attractive firepits and fireplaces complement the landscaping and architecture of the houses they accompany. You can install an outdoor fireplace or firepit in a sheltered patio, along the rear wall of a home, or at the boundary between paved and planted areas. In fact, in the proper location a fireplace can add wind protection and privacy to a patio.

Traditional masonry models—with a firebrick-lined firebox, and a brick-lined or stone chimney—are heavy and expensive. But lighter, less-expensive options are available, including precast modules that stack together to make firebox, fireplace, and chimney. For portability, opt for metal firepits or *chimeneas* (freestanding fireplaces made of clay).

In the dry Southwest, common sense dictates that you take extra care with fireplaces. Chimneys should include spark arresters—screens that prevent large embers from escaping.

top A portable copper firepit warms this contemporary outdoor room. Repeating the fire's warmth is the semicircle of crenellated wall, painted in soft golden orange and edged with seatwalls of hot pink and lavender blue. left A dramatic earthenware bowl hosts a flickering fire at dusk in a Southwest patio. Ideal for outdoor entertaining, the fiery presence gives guests a visual focal point as well as a warming place to congregate when the evening chill descends.

below Brick-hued tiles and earth-toned plastered adobe form an outdoor fireplace in the style of native pueblos. It's a good spot for congregating on nippy evenings: the wide hearth doubles as a spacious seating area while the firebox opens on two sides to spread its bounty of warmth.

above This peaceful bed of black Mexican beach pebbles enclosed by a pale geometric border holds a surprise: a gas firepit that needs only a touch of ignition to burst into flames and warm the evening air.

A medieval-looking massive steel cauldron holds a roaring fire that casts its warmth over a well-lit patio and adjacent garden. With its dramatic appearance and promise of comfort, this fire feature offers compelling reasons to linger outdoors long after the sun has set.

right A brightly colored fire-place is designed for evening entertainment. From a dip in the pool at the right, guests can migrate to warm them-selves around a welcoming fire, where the hearth and built-in bench merge into one spacious seating area. below "Come gather 'round while I tell you a story." This cozy patio scene is the perfect setting for huddling close to the fire, listening to yarns of the Old West. With a portable firepot such as this, you can easily put together an inviting conversation group wherever you please.

above A cherry-red curved seat wall defines this outdoor spot—something of a glorified sandbox—complete with firepit to ward off the chill. It's also perfect for a picnic, with hot dogs and marshmallows toasted on the fire.

above Beauty and comfort meld in a welcoming outdoor room that features a bed clothed in Native American weavings, groups of Mexican *equipale* chairs, a generous *chimenea*-style fireplace, and a brick floor softened with throw rugs. left With fire blazing, this pit looks like a ground-level volcanic crater. But when flames subside to glowing coals, the grill spanning it is ready to receive all manner of barbecue treats from steaks to humble burgers—for enjoyment from the comfy bench seat just beyond.

OUTDOOR FURNITURE REMINDS US THAT A GARDEN IS NOT ONLY A PLACE TO WEED AND WORK BUT ALSO A PLACE TO REST, REFLECT, DINE, AND ENTERTAIN.

furniture

There's an enduring graciousness to outdoor furniture with a Southwest flavor—the faded and weathered turquoise-painted benches, the traditional Mexican *equipale* chairs made of rawhide with woven wood bases that sit so well in adobe-walled court-yards. But you might instead choose whimsical furnishings painted in primary colors of red, yellow, blue, and green, or sleek contemporary chairs and lounges in soft earth tones. Some "furnishings" aren't portable at all but rather built into low walls for bonus seating and lounging.

Choose your furnishings as much for comfort as for durability and style; you can scatter colorful cushions on stucco seat walls, for example. Position lounge chairs to face great views across the desert or to draw people toward a glowing fireplace; place benches along paths in tree-shaded corners of your garden.

Here's the ultimate built-in: an outdoor couch growing out of an adobe and stucco retaining wall. Puffy cushions and a soft, mattresslike seat ensure a comfortable visit; maintenance of the bench itself is minimal—just the occasional coat of paint.

above Simplicity is the essence of traditional Southwest furniture, including outdoor pieces. Here, straightforward planks of pine are used in a no-frills bench design, only a wash of blue paint serving as decoration. Equally simple are the two tables: stone slabs mounted on log sections. left Startling Southwest motifs in bright colors decorate a wooden bench. Furthering the bold design, a Navajo rug made from natural-dye yarns is spread over the seat. The neutral-colored stucco wall showcases the ensemble as a work of art.

top left A simple coating of light teal blue paint puts a new face on this vintage icebox. Its refrigeration days long gone, it now functions as a storage chest and is the centerpiece in a varied display of Southwest folk-art objects. bottom left The hammock—a New World contribution to outdoor creature comfort—gets a modern upgrade in ultramarine blue canvas. And what better place to suspend the relaxation station than from the posts of a shaded but airy pergola?

GATES HAVE AN OBVIOUS PRACTICAL PURPOSE, BUT THERE'S NO REASON THEY NEED TO BE DULL. INSTEAD, THINK OF GATES AS OPPORTUNITIES FOR GARDEN ART.

gates

From first-impression entry portals to humbler garden separators, gates are natural focal points. The prevalence of walls (see page 169) in Southwest tradition has spawned a rich development of artistic gates. Some, mimicking Spanish-colonial cathedral doors, are imposing creations of weathered wood with decorative carving; simpler versions—without decoration—are no less impressive for their sheer heft and air of antiquity. Add a wash of colorful paint and you create a fusion of traditional style with contemporary verve. In gardens where privacy is less of an issue, artistic ingenuity has inspired fabrication of wildly varied ironwork gates. Indigenous tradition is captured in constructions resembling wattles, made from native ocotillo stems.

top This portal's inspiration is the classic Asian moon gate, but here the design has an unmistakable Southwest flavor. Rugged native stones tie the structure to the surrounding landscape, while the wrought iron gate itself celebrates the region with stylized renderings of three familiar native plants: agave, palo verde, and saguaro. left A plain stucco wall comes alive when a simple wooden gate painted brilliant blue becomes a focal point, beside a curtain of Boston ivy.

below Passage through this massive, rough adobe-and-plaster wall is guarded by a filigree ironwork gate in a style clearly tracing to Spain via Mexico. Its spiderweb openness affords tantalizing glimpses of the thriving garden.

above Carefully crafted like a piece of fine furniture, this natural-finish wooden gate makes an elegant "front door" entry to a spacious flagstone patio; the gate's warm wood tones are set off by twilight-colored adobe walls painted to harmonize with the patio paving.

right Salvaged wooden panels, their original painted surfaces left to weather into washy gray tones, fit together in an unadorned stucco wall to form a perpetually open gate watched over by a faux-primitive ritual mask.

right Captured in golden metal in this fanciful gate is the essence of the California and Arizona low desert: an ever-present, radiant stylized sun beats down on a sculptural rendition of the region's signature Joshua tree.

above In this Grand Entrance, the earth-toned adobe walls embrace a gateway worthy of a cathedral. The elaborately carved wooden panels painted cobalt blue have a weathered look to indicate venerable age.

left Although the scale of this gate is smaller than that of the one above, its similar blue paint washed with white still makes a striking statement. Here it ushers you into a flower-filled garden; when closed, the gate's brilliant blue makes a telling contrast to the pink and white blossoms.

above Use color both to define and to direct. In this entrance, cobalt blue paint decorates a wooden gate, a window shutter, and associated trim, drawing attention to the two breaches in the plain gray-lilac stucco wall.

SOUTHWEST STYLE

walls

SOUTHWEST GARDENS ABOUND WITH WALLS THAT ENCLOSE OR SEPARATE OUTDOOR LIVING AREAS EFFECTIVELY AND ATTRACTIVELY, OFTEN ADDING A DISTINCT REGIONAL FLAVOR.

Traditional Southwest architecture is all about thick, earthen walls that form building exteriors and delineate boundaries. The region's original building material was native clay (adobe), producing walls that appeared to grow from the surrounding soil. From pueblo to Spanish cathedral to courtyard, such walls established an essential Southwest "look"—one that implied stability, security, and a bit of mystery.

In today's desert landscapes, traditional-style walls that look rooted in nature firmly tie a garden to the surrounding terrain. But contemporary designers have spun variations on tradition. Walls may retain the simple, blank-slate look of old adobe but have a coating of stucco or plaster for a more finished surface. Their featureless facades invite ornamentation by sculpture, niches, and decorative tiles. Strategically placed windows break the sense of enclosure to offer tantalizing glimpses of the natural landscape beyond. And daring designers have created dazzling effects by painting the walls in vibrant Southwest colors.

top A low stucco wall, rising to surround a carved wood gate, separates garden areas without obscuring one from another. The neutral color and rounded edges reflect regional adobe tradition. above Starkly modern designs use walls as features. Not only do they enclose a shimmering pool here, but they also form bands of color to contrast with the water. A solitary barrel cactus highlights the prevailing angularity. right Like a throwback in time, this unadorned adobe-and-stone wall with arched portal appears ready to receive riders on horseback.

NOTHING CREATES AMBIANCE MORE SUCCESSFULLY THAN BEAUTIFUL LIGHTING.
ON WARM EVENINGS, LIGHTS DRAW YOU INTO THE GARDEN TO ENJOY THE
FRESHNESS OF THE LANDSCAPE.

lights

When night falls, each spot, beam, and soft wash of light accentuates
your garden's focal points—whether a stately saguaro, a sculpture, or
a wall fountain. Permanent lighting fixtures have a practical use: to outline
paths and steps for safe and easy walking. But festive occasions and outdoor
parties sometimes call for portable lighting to supplement the usual sources
of illumination.

A broad range of lanterns is available, from hurricane lamps that burn oil
to glass-sided lanterns that house candles. Classic New Mexican luminarias
—open paper bags that contain votives set in sand—are simple and elegant
lined up along an adobe wall and glowing softly against a winter sky. Strings
of mini-lights laced around a trellis or arbor turn a backyard into a festive
palace for a party. And lanterns on stakes can add drama to a path or gate.

above Lights in key locations keep this expansive pool patio illuminated discreetly. The exterior of a rear wall is highlighted by a fixture behind a pillar; lights behind windows and beneath the pool coping illuminate the pool area; and a firepit casts a warm glow at one corner of the water.

facing page In a Hollywood lighting treatment, the swimming pool is illuminated by two torchieres, their images repeated in the blue-black water. Underwater lights in the inflow channel compete with a reflection of the fire platform. The coral-colored backdrop is kept aglow by concealed ground-level lights. above Traditional luminarias get a new twist: small and large star cutouts in the bags let the candle glow sparkle though. right Chunky candles—on holders of various heights and sitting in a niche—wash this wall with a warm glow.

COLOR IS A POWERFUL DESIGN TOOL, MOST OFTEN INTRODUCED TO A GARDEN WITH FLOWERS OR ACCESSORIES SUCH AS TILES. BUT PAINT CAN ACHIEVE REMARKABLE RESULTS ON ITS OWN.

paint

Used with care, colored walls and structures can give a garden a larger or smaller appearance. Bright, warm hues, such as orange and red, make an outdoor space vibrate with excitement; cool blues, grays, or greens create a sense of calm. In this region where the sun is bright and desert blooms are subtle, painted walls add drama to courtyards and gardens. You can use colored walls as backdrops for plants. For simplicity, choose the same flower and paint colors—a bright yellow wall behind a billowy planting of yellow desert marigolds. Or choose a different but closely related color: a stucco wall painted dusty lavender behind a soft blue-green *Opuntia*. Don't be afraid to try a bold hue; if you don't like it, you can always paint over it.

Color rules in this patio, and paint sets the tone. A stepped-down wall in neon-bright cerise compels attention to itself and the pool below, framed in ultramarine. Such vivid colors demand equally bright accents: red chaise and hammock cushions, red, orange, and yellow flowers.

right Try to picture this scene with the coral wall in a neutral tone like the one behind it, and you'll appreciate how paint can enliven and define a space. The sweep of lively color separates one wall from the other, makes a striking statement, and complements nature's green palette.

above Color harmony is safe—and effective. The window framing boasts a coat of true blue paint, the base color for this scheme. Add a bit of pink to blue and you get lavender—the soft hue covering the plain stucco wall. Bougainvilea blossoms of violet—blue plus red—round out the picture. right This carefully nuanced composition proves that monochrome schemes can be anything but dull. Each different blue stands out from the others by virtue of its color depth or the addition of other tints to alter the tone.

An eye-catching but soft blue accentuates the whimsy of these stylized shark fins, placed like an improbable armada-on-the-move in a garden of drought-tolerant plants.

below In a compelling color somewhere between coral and cherry, this painted wall unquestionably defines the herb garden's boundary, makes a striking backdrop, and posts a contemporary update of a traditional gardening motto.

The best place to find God is in a garden.
You can dig for Him there.

Traditional terra-cotta pots would have competed for attention with the cacti and succulents in this assemblage. But painting the pots in blue shades, a stroke of genius, picks up the blue cast in the plants, harmonizing the containers with their contents.

USING COLOR

Walls of dusty pink, pale lavender, sky blue, coral, rose pink, and turquoise have their place under the desert sun—they echo the hues of a Southwest sky at twilight, and they make beautiful backdrops for spring flowers and soft green plants like cacti. Rich reds, purple, and cobalt blue can also be used—sparingly—to add visual punch to gardens. Here are more ways to awaken your garden with color.

◈ FOCAL POINTS Paint a rich jewel tone—say, sapphire blue—on a single wing wall or a square section of wall that backs a small square pool. Then plant a scarlet bougainvillea to billow along the top of the wall.

◈ ACCENTS Use bright ribbons of color to outline wall-mounted fountains, gates, seat walls, outdoor fireplaces, even windows and doors. Paint a gate or a pair of chairs in a vivid hue; setting them at the end of a pool or path will draw your eye to them. Or, for bright moments of color, build a cluster of small stucco pyramids in a sea of decomposed granite, and paint them cornflower blue.

◈ DIVERSIONS Paint the wall of a small, sunny side yard a pretty color, and then set an urn or a row of sculptural cacti in front of it. A highly colored wall can draw attention away from an unattractive view.

◈ DIVIDERS Paint a freestanding masonry wall a vivid lemon yellow, dusty pink, or sky blue. Outdoor room dividers, like indoor ones, can add color and drama.

WITH CONTEMPORARY EMPHASIS ON THE GARDEN AS AN EXTERIOR ROOM, OUTDOOR PAVING HAS BECOME AN INTEGRAL AND DECORATIVE PART OF GARDEN DESIGN.

paving

Current pavement options go way beyond concrete and dirt. Nowadays, selecting outdoor paving can be just as complex and inspiring as shopping for interior floor coverings. Opportunities abound for you to coordinate paving with your overall home and garden design. Particularly suited to southwestern settings are regional specialties such as terra-cotta tiles, native stones, adobe pavers, and gravel surfaces. For more elaborate artistic expressions, you can celebrate regional design traditions in aggregate-pebble surfaces or mosaic tiles. And, of course, there's no need to limit your garden to just a single pavement: exciting designs can result from combining two (or more) different types. All this is not to say, though, that the original two materials are passé. Once-pedestrian concrete has metamorphosed from gray slab to art form, thanks to imaginative tinting, staining, and forming; outdoors, its durability is still unsurpassed. And ubiquitous bare earth is the ultimate "natural" surface, completely in harmony with the environment and very appropriate in some settings.

By using paving sparingly, you create the impression of house and garden springing directly from the surrounding desert. Here, a precisely delineated patio sits in a naturalistic sea of gravel punctuated by indigenous stones leading into the landscape. Carefully chosen and sited grasses appear to have grown naturally among the stones.

above Natural materials like these large flagstones make a handsome and durable patio floor. Gravel fills the spaces between them, and water-sculpted rocks form a ribbon of dry streambed in the foreground.

above Irregular flagstones make a transition from the geometric steps and wall to the softer gravel hardscape in this garden.
left A progression of rectangular concrete pavers leaves no doubt about where you're supposed to walk, on this path past a cool urn fountain. But their staggered placement and the imprecise edges of the surrounding gravel give the pathway a riverlike sense of flow through the area.

IN THE SUN-DRENCHED SOUTHWEST, OUTDOOR SHADE STRUCTURES LET YOU
ROAM OUT OF THE HOUSE TO ENJOY THE GARDEN AT CLOSE RANGE IN COMFORT.

shade
structures

When nature denies you trees, you turn to structures for relief
from the sun. Ingenious Southwest natives long ago developed
the ramada, still an excellent structure for beating the heat
(see sidebar). If you lack traditional ramada-making materials,
adapt the concept to suit what's available. Timbers, fabric
(canvas is durable), and woven matting all can serve—individually or in
combination—as overhead sunscreens. Freestanding structures lure you
away from the house into the garden, where they offer shady retreat.
You can also take a cue from Mexican-Spanish courtyards and make the
shaded area an extension of the house; this is especially useful on southern
and western exposures. Even a simple vine-draped arbor can do the job,
giving outdoor shade as well as cooling the house wall behind it.

above This classic ramada is charming and effective. The uprights and roof supports are tree
trunks; on top, closely spaced branches create shade. Three sides are open for air circulation, but
on the afternoon-sun side a screen of ocotillo sticks filters light and lets breezes through.

THE RAMADA

Do any structures that provide shade from the hottest sun capture the spirit of the Southwest more fully than ramadas? Original ramadas were twiggy shelters—open on three sides to let the breezes blow through—that Native Americans used as work stations for doing jobs like food preparation and leathercraft. Most often they were built of natural materials such as mesquite or cottonwood poles and ocotillo ribs. But contemporary ramadas are more permanent structures, either freestanding or attached to houses, that extend living space outdoors during the seasons when it's pleasant to be in the open air. They're used mostly for leisure—coffee and newspapers on Sunday mornings, cocktails before dinner on weekday evenings, places where you can pause and enjoy the garden.

How you use the ramada determines how you equip it. For lounging in its shade, either by the pool or in a corner of the garden, you can outfit it simply with deck chairs. Canvas or split bamboo shades offer protection from low-angled sun. A ceiling fan increases air circulation and cools the structure on warm, still days. For nighttime use, some kind of lighting—either electric lights or portable lanterns—is essential. A table and chairs convert a ramada into an outdoor dining room. For a complete entertaining area, you can install a barbecue, fireplace, refrigerator, wet bar, and cabinets.

below Fit for a desert sheik is this canvas awning supported above an entry door by two wrought-iron staffs. Because the canvas intercepts sunlight only from directly above, its shadow will shift position throughout the day.

above Like a detached room, this shade structure takes its design cue from the ramada but casts it, literally, in stone. Local rocks link the structure to its site, while the metal roof guarantees total shade as well as shelter from the occasional downpour. The substantial chimney is evidence of a fireplace for evening warmth.

above Simple, attractive fabric panels strung from wall to opposite wall above this quiet courtyard shade the dining area below. right Canvas "sails," looking like abstract birds coming in for a landing, are suspended by wires above a sunny outdoor living area. The triangles are carefully positioned so that they continue to cast shadow over the patio as the sun moves through the sky.

right A "house-bound" ramada executed in craftsman style, this airy shaded space invites you to relax outside in comfort. Permanent columns support a wooden roof. The built-in fireplace provides welcome warmth for extending use into chilly evenings. below An arbor adorned with bougainvillea leads to an outdoor sitting area beneath a roof extension from the main house. Although totally protected overhead from sun and rain, the space is exposed on three sides to take advantage of cooling breezes.

above A four-post, freestanding arbor shelters a current version of the old-fashioned glider, perfect for a relaxing swing in the shade while savoring the breeze and the view of California poppies. Borrowing from the ramada, three sides are open but a high wall behind blocks the strongest prevailing wind.

WATER IS A SOUTHWEST GARDEN'S MAGIC INGREDIENT. ADD A BIT OF IT, AND YOU IMMEDIATELY LIFT THE GARDEN MOOD AND SEEM TO TAKE THE EDGE OFF THE HEAT.

water features

Valuable commodity that water is in arid regions, no wonder water-scarce cultures both conserve and celebrate it. In the Southwest, Native Americans developed elaborate water channels for irrigating crops; the imported Spanish-Moorish-Persian tradition added pools and fountains for purely aesthetic and spiritual pleasure. Today's Southwest gardens incorporate water both for visual delight and for the cooling effect it provides as a contrast to the region's hot climate. Just the sight of a pool or channel of still water is soothing; and, even when out of view, the very sound of water from a fountain, or spilling from one pool to another, conveys its moist coolness. Remember that using more water doesn't necessarily equal a cooler effect—just a small pool, a sliver of water, or even a single jet of a fountain can do the trick.

This bougainvillea-wreathed water feature in Moorish-Persian tradition could easily be from a courtyard in southern Spain or Mexico. Through a clay pipe in a simple plastered wall, a small stream of water spills into three successively larger pools, the melodic splash of moving water adding to the sense of coolness.

above Frankly contemporary in design, this water-enhanced patio is in harmony with the rugged, hard-edged terrain beyond its boundaries. Water contained in the narrow raised pool at left spills in a slender ribbon to the larger pool at ground level.

above A very different water feature in the Moorish-Persian style has a stream of water sluicing down the rear garden wall and then conveyed in this narrow channel to a central square pool. left Three ceramic vessels, glazed brilliant blue, serve as bubbling fountains spilling into a shallow, glacially white pool. At pool's edge and in the background, two more blue jugs link pool and landscape.

left In a stylized adaptation of geometric Persian pleasure gardens, two square pools, raised to seat height, feed water channels through the formal landscape. above A generous swimming pool is a dramatic feature. Here, the water's surface creates an impressionistic reflection of the surrounding cherry-colored walls, grayed grasses, and warm pink paving—mingled with blue from the pool's depths. below This free-form swimming pool is designed in desert-oasis style. Native stone paving surrounds it, boulders from the site impinge on the far side, and native plants—including signature oasis palms—embrace the pool from the background.

top left Sparkling with little white lights, a colony of native saguaros rises out of the desert landscape like an alien welcoming committee of sorts. As twilight gives way to night, the cacti stand out as beacons in the darkness. top right Almost like the path to Oz: parallel strands of tiny, ice-blue lights create the illusion of a flowing stream leading the eye through the darkened landscape to the dramatically lit red walls of the distant compound.

above Lacking holly or evergreen boughs, southwesterners use ingenuity and regional materials. Pads of beavertail cactus form a holiday wreath with a cape of dried chilis and a rosette-form succulent—dried and gilded—on top. right When snow comes to high-elevation Southwest areas, it creates impromptu decorations. Here, snow-encrusted tree branches frame a wood door with iron accents and a white-flocked festive dried-chile wreath.

resources

arizona

THE ARBORETUM AT FLAGSTAFF

4001 South Woody Mountain Road, Flagstaff, AZ 86001

(928) 774-1442; www.thearb.org

Open daily April 1–December 15. Situated on the Colorado Plateau, at an elevation above 7,000 feet, this peaceful setting is suffused with the fresh scent of ponderosa pine. More than 2,500 plant species provide seasonal color along several miles of groomed trails. Summer is particularly spectacular, with penstemon, columbine, and skyrocket brightening the wildflower meadows. Check out the passive solar greenhouse and aromatic herb garden.

ARIZONA-SONORA DESERT MUSEUM

2021 North Kinney Road, Tucson, AZ 85743

(520) 883-2702; www.desertmuseum.org

Open daily. This botanical garden, zoo, and natural history museum all rolled into one is an ideal place for exploring the region's plants, animals, and geology. More than 1,400 plant species and 300 animal species are found on-site, including 20 that are endangered or threatened. Exhibits re-create the animals' native Sonoran Desert habitat so that you can view them in natural surroundings. The museum also researches important environmental issues such as the migratory patterns of pollinators.

BAKER NURSERY

3414 North 40th Street, Phoenix, AZ 85018

(602) 955-4500; www.bakernurseryaz.com

Open daily. Jim Baker started this nursery more than 35 years ago, offering desert-adapted plants before "xeriscape" was a buzzword. Three generations of Bakers now share their expertise. Jim, in his 80s, still offers tours on his golf cart, pausing to chat with longtime customers or show a detail under a magnifying loupe. You'll enjoy shopping for low-water landscape plants as well as annuals, perennials, houseplants, bulbs, seeds, containers, and garden ornaments.

BOYCE THOMPSON ARBORETUM

37615 U.S. Highway 60, Superior, AZ 85273

(520) 689-2723; http://arboretum.ag.arizona.edu

Open daily. Discover the diverse plant life thriving just an hour from Phoenix. Towering eucalyptus and shade canopies parallel the Queen Creek habitat. Volcanic magma hills are thick with saguaro, jojoba, and other desert plants. Near the herb garden is a stone dwelling from the early 1900s that housed a whole family in the space of a modern master bathroom. Demonstration gardens offer creative ideas you can translate to your outdoor living spaces.

DESERT BOTANICAL GARDEN

1201 North Galvin Parkway, Phoenix, AZ 85008

(480) 941-1225; www.dbg.org

Open daily, except July 4 and Christmas. This nonprofit garden has a guaranteed showing of spring wildflowers. The People and Plants of the Sonoran Desert Trail features hands-on exhibits about the traditional uses of native plants. Try your skill at grinding mesquite beans into flour with a stone metate or twisting agave fibers into rope. Don't miss the Marshall Butterfly Pavilion in spring. In-the-know plant lovers queue hours in advance for the semiannual sales, jockeying to be first to snag hard-to-find species.

GARDEN TERRITORY

6106 South 32nd Street, Phoenix, AZ 85042

(602) 268-1962; www.gardenterritory.com

Call for hours. Master gardener Leslie Honaker and holistic nutrition educator Terri Nacke are self-described "barn goddesses" who have refurbished a rustic stable tucked into the corner of a pecan orchard. Set among towering hollyhocks and seasonal wildflowers, and featuring a shady porch with comfy sofas, their business offers classes in desert gardening, seasonal cooking, and nutrition. The enthusiastic duo stock an eclectic assortment of organically grown herbs and bedding plants, vintage garden décor, botanical paintings, and their own line of aromatherapy products.

GLENDALE XERISCAPE BOTANICAL GARDEN

Glendale Main Library

5959 West Brown Street, Glendale, AZ 85302

(623) 930-3596; www.glendaleaz.com

Open daily. Books aren't the only things to check out at the Glendale Library. Its grounds host the Glendale Xeriscape Botanical Garden, a hidden gem displaying more than 400 desert-adapted plant species in one easy-viewing locale. Pick up an audio wand in the library to enjoy a one-hour, self-guided garden tour. Be sure to grab a copy of "Tales from the Garden" in the lobby. This free booklet covers area history and provides photos and descriptions of drought-tolerant plants.

NATIVE SEEDS/SEARCH

5527 North 4th Avenue, Tucson, AZ 85705

(520) 622-5561; www.nativeseeds.org

Open daily. This nonprofit organization protects crop diversity by conserving and distributing native crop seeds of the southwestern United States and northwestern Mexico. Its seed bank houses 2,000 varieties representing 99 species grown or used by tribes in the region. On its southern Arizona farm, hundreds of crops are grown annually to replenish seed stock. The group promotes traditional desert foods to combat diabetes, a scourge in Native American communities. Seeds, food products such as tepary beans and mesquite flour, and native crafts are sold. Inquire about free seed for Native Americans.

PLANTS FOR THE SOUTHWEST

50 East Blacklidge, Tucson, AZ 85705

(520) 628-8773; www.lithops.com

Open Wednesdays–Saturdays. Plant collectors Jane Evans and Gene Joseph are on hand to offer growing advice about their intriguing selection of cacti and succulents, such as *Dyckia*, *Haworthia*, and the diminutive *Lithops*, commonly called "living rocks." Look for the artistically designed container gardens in the first greenhouse. Local artists display their pottery periodically, providing a perfect opportunity to match unique containers and plant specimens.

TERA'S GARDEN

606 North 4th Avenue, Phoenix, AZ 85003

(602) 253-4744; www.terasgarden.com

Call for hours. Master gardener Tera Vessels renovated a house in the Roosevelt Historic District, turning it into a charming source of garden-themed ornaments, home décor, jewelry, hats, houseplants, bulbs, tools, and containers. The yard overflows with landscape and bedding plants, uncommon perennials, water features, and original sculpture and metalwork. The sidewalk medians double as demonstration gardens.

TOHONO CHUL PARK

7366 North Paseo del Norte, Tucson, AZ 85704

(520) 742-6455; www.tohonochulpark.org

Open daily. The park's teahouse is a delightful spot to take out-of-town guests for breakfast, lunch, or afternoon tea. Then view desert plants in native settings along the Saguaro Discovery Trail or in the Hummingbird, Sin Agua (water harvesting), and Riparian gardens. Monitor the park Web site for the annual night-blooming cereus event sometime in May or June. Flashlight-toting visitors troop along the trails to locate dozens of these fragrant cactus blooms. In July 2004, work began on the Desert Living Courtyard, a section designed to model landscape techniques and provide easy-to-replicate xeriscape plans.

desert california

THE LIVING DESERT ZOO AND GARDENS

47-900 Portola Avenue, Palm Desert, CA 92260

(760) 346-5694; www.livingdesert.org

Open daily. All deserts are not equal! You'll see this as you stroll through North American and African desert habitats reproduced with plants and wildlife distinct to specific regions, such as the Sonoran, Mojave, Upper Colorado, or Madagascar deserts. The Wortz Demonstration Garden features Southwest native plants useful in landscapes. If you want to soak up more desert ambience, head for the trails on the 1,000-acre wilderness preserve.

nevada

THE GARDENS AT THE SPRINGS PRESERVE

3701 West Alta Drive, Las Vegas, NV 89153

(702) 258-3205; www.springspreserve.org

Open daily; call for master gardener hours. This charming desert demonstration garden is an excellent resource for homeowners who want to create or tend a low-water landscape. It features 2.5 acres of waterwise plants and design ideas, as well as classes on xeric landscape construction and maintenance. Master gardener volunteers answer questions on-site two days each week. A planned expansion will incorporate museum galleries, a trail system, an outdoor amphitheater, an indoor theater, and a desert living center.

new mexico

AGUA FRIA NURSERY

1409 Agua Fria, Santa Fe, NM 87505

(505) 983-4831; aguafrianr@aol.com

Call for hours. Owner Bob Pennington is a native plant expert, selling treasures that you won't find elsewhere. This third-generation full-service nursery cultivates native plants grown from seed, often hand-collected. Pennington offers an astounding variety of more than 100 *Penstemon* species, and he admits that an equal mania for *Eriogonum* is in development.

BERNARDO BEACH NATIVE PLANTS

3729 Arno Street NE, Albuquerque, NM 87107-2201

(505) 345-6248; no Web site

Call for hours. Owners Judith and Roland Phillips grow native and climate-adapted plants suited to specific ecosystems and growing conditions, such as high desert, foothills, riparian areas, or clay soil in valleys. Judith is the author of several books on native plants and Southwest landscape design, so it's no wonder the nursery displays plants in groups, rather than straight rows. This encourages gardeners to picture how plants would look together in their own landscape setting.

RIO GRANDE BOTANIC GARDEN

2601 Central Avenue NW, Albuquerque, NM 87104

(505) 764-6200;

www.cabq.gov/biopark/garden/#general

Open daily. A beautiful modern glass conservatory houses desert and Mediterranean plant collections. Walled gardens, such as the Spanish-Moorish Court, pay homage to Old World design. But it's the Children's Fantasy Garden that will draw you in, no matter how many decades are under your belt. A 14-foot-tall topiary dragon looms near the entry, which is a giant rabbit hole. Look for humongous potted plants, bird eggs, carrots, and pinecones. A delightful bonus for summer visitors, the PNM Butterfly Pavilion exhibits hundreds of North American butterflies from May through September.

SANTA FE GREENHOUSES

2904 Rufina Street, Santa Fe, New Mexico 87507-2929

(505) 473-2700; www.santafegreenhouses.com (retail location); www.highcountrygardens.com (online sales)

Open daily; call for tour times. Owner David Salman is a long-term advocate of waterwise planting, offering trees, shrubs, ground covers, grasses, and perennials adapted to arid lands, since 1984. New selections, tested in Santa Fe's demanding growing conditions, are continually introduced for sale. The half-acre demonstration gardens brim with colorful, drought-tolerant plants that are magnets for hummingbirds and butterflies. If you're confused by all the choices, prepared plant combinations eliminate guesswork.

photography credits

Doug Baldwin: *90B*; Christian Blok: *32B, 94T, 95T, B, 96, 110, 179L*; Nicola Browne: *133TL, 180T*; Linda Burgess/Alamy: *151BR, 175T*; Gay Bumgarner/Positive Images: *133L*; Karen Bussolini: *106BL, 127T, 134, 167TR*; Andrew Cattoir: *33R*; David Cavagnaro: *125BR*; Stephen Cridland: *144*; Claire Curran: *65R, 82TR, 107BR, 148, 149TR*; Lisl Dennis: *3BR, 41TR, 77T, 105TR, 171CL*; Jack Dykinga: *2BL, 4BL, 5BL, 17, 19, 63BR, 92, 105TL, 167BR, 187TR, 192*; Clay Ellis: *35TL*; Linda Enger: *39, 47, 75B, 87TR, BR, 156BL, 163B, 167TL, 177BL, BR, 184TR*; David Golberg/Susan A. Roth & Co.: *125BL*; Jeff Green: *4BR, 10, 24, 61TR, 89TL, 114, 170*; Steven Gunther: *22, 32T, 35BR, 63T, 65BL, 69 all, 70 all, 71, 78, 82BL, 85, 109, 112, 116CL, CR, 121B, 123 all, 129TR, 169T, 179R, 184BR, 185BR*; Jamie Hadley: *113TL*; Jerry Harpur: *6, 49, 115TL, 122, 150*; Marcus Harpur: *145*; H. Ross Hawkins: *86*; Saxon Holt: *113R, 136TL, 149B*; George H. H. Huey: *4–5T, 4BC, 5BR, 12, 25B, 34BR, 59B, 60TR, 84L, 87TL, 106, 156BR*; Stephen Ingram: *106BR, 115CR*; Catherine Karnow: *175B*; Tom Krebsbach: *163T, 171B*; Elliot Lincis: *58B, 61B*; Richard Maack: *33L, 161TL, 171T, 183T*; Charles Mann: *2, 25T, 40, 41BR, 50BL, 54B, 60TL, 94B, 99B, 100B, 101 all, 104, 106BC, 116TL, TR, B, 118 all, 119B, 121TR, 127B, 128, 129 all, 130T, 131T, 131BR, 132, 133BL, 135L, BR, 136R, BL, BC, 137TR, B, 138TL, 139, 140L, 141, 142, 143L, 146, 147L, R, 150BL, 151BL, 153, 154–155 all, 156TL, 157B, 159TL, 164, 165TR, BR, 166B, 167BL, 168 all, 169B, 173L, 174 all, 181BR, 183BL, BR, 184TL, 185L, 187BR*; Buddy Mays/Travel Stock: *187TL*; Edward McCain: *186*; J. B. McCarthy: *76B*; Terrence Moore: *2BR, 26, 37T, 50T, 55R, 57B, 58T, 72–73 all, 93B, 97 all, 99T, 117T, 130BL, 150BR, 156TR, 162T, 166T, 169C, 172, 177T, 178, 181T, 185TR*; Daniel Nadelbach: *34BL, 37B, 41L, 46TL, 56, 60B, 65T, 77B, 90T, 98 all, 100T, 102 all, 103T, 133BR, 163T*; Jerry Pavia: *124, 133TR*; Victoria Pearson/Botanica: *75T*; Norman A. Plate: *1, 20, 23, 26BL, BC, BR, 27BL, 28–31 all, 35TR, 36, 38 all, 42–45 all, 46TR, 46B, 48, 51, 53, 54T, 57T, 59L, TR, 62, 64, 67, 68, 76T, 79 all, 81 all, 89BR, 108, 111TL, 115B, 117B, 125T, 126, 130BR, 135TR, 138B, 149TL, 152, 157T, 158, 159TR, BR, 161TR, 162BR, 165TL, BL, 173TR, 180B, 181BL, 187BL*; Steven J. Prchal: *87BL*; Randy A. Prentice: *107BL, 111TR, BL, BR*; Susan A. Roth: *3BL, 119T, 121TL, 137TL, 140R, 143R, 159CR*; France Ruffenach: *55B*; William J. Salman: *83B, 103B*; Jeremy Samuelson/Botanica: *27BR, 74*; Kim Sayer/Garden Picture Library: *120*; Paul and Mary Schweiker: *80B*; Richard Shiell: *129BL*; J. Scott Smith: *93T*; Dave Souers: *91R*; Thomas J. Story: *160T, 182*; Tim Street-Porter/Botanica: *150BC, 162BL, 173BR*; Ron Sutherland/Alamy: *176*; Christopher Talbot Frank: *14*; Michael S. Thompson: *131BL*; E. Spencer Toy: *13*; John Trotto: *160B, 161B*; Larry Ulrich: *105B*; Dominique Vorillon: *88*; Andy Wasowski: *52L*; judywhite/GardenPhotos.com: *113B, 159BL*; James Wilson: *80TL, TR*; Karen Witynsky: *34T*

garden design credits

Patrick Anderson: *35BR*; Antique Rose Emporium: *167TR*; Arterra: *39*; Mark and Jan Barmann/John Harlow Jr.: *26–27T*; Julia Berman: *135BR*; Susan Blevins: *40, 41BR, 181BR*; Marcus Bollinger: *54T, 92*; Michael Buccino: *22, 121B, 181T, 184BR*; Debra Burnette, Steve Martino, and J. Barry Moffett: *110*; Kevin Casey and Ken Bowling: *93B*; Dan Cauldillo: *99B, 146, 168BR*; Steve Chase: *6*; Chip-N-Dale's Custom Landscaping: *65BL*; Peter Cure: *166T*; Topher Delaney: *160T*; Desert Custom Lighting: *187TR*; Doug Diggins: *79T*; Stephen K. Domigan: *101B*; John Douglas: *183T*; Tyler Gerdes: *68*; Greey/Pickett Partners: *82TR*; Dave Hansen Enterprises (shower rock): *92*; Michelle Hearon: *185TR*; Debra Huffman: *58T*; Raquel Hughes Design: *159TL*; Terry Jones/Xiascapes: *58BL*; Margaret Joplin: *111TL*; Cory Kelso/David Larkins: *69B*; Landscaping by André: *84–85*; Little and Lewis/Lauren Springer: *106BL, 134*; Hal Lowe: *32L*; Jean Manocchio: *135TR*; Leslie Mansur/Great Gardens: *37T*; Steve Martino: *150BL, 154BL, 174T, 180T*; Melissa McDonald: *2–3T*; Judy McGowan: *42–43 all*; Keeyla Meadows: *157T*; Mesa Design Group: *80TL, TR*; Gilda Meyer-Niehof (stylist): *34BL, 37B, 41L, 46TL, 56, 60B, 65T, 77B, 90T, 98 all, 100T, 102 all, 103T, 133BR, 163T*; John Mikiska/Star Masonry: *99T*; Rodney Mott: *156TR*; Carrie Nimmer: *46TR, 81T, 94B, 141, 155BR*; Noble Design Studio: *76B*; Faith Okuma: *57B*; Faith Okuma, Design Workshop: *2BR, 97 all*; Diana Osborne (architect): *185TR*; Dan Overbeck: *26BL, 28–31 all*; Brian Patterson: *61TR*; Anthony Paul: *176*; Corky Poster: *117B*; Janet Rademacker: *155TR, 162BR, 165TL*; Chad Robert: *46B, 64, 173TR*; Steven Rogers: *59L*; Steven Rogers and Mike Ferraro, Sonoran Desert Designs: *36*; Steven Rogers, Sonoran Desert Design: *48*; Cyndy Scanlon: *1, 26BR, 44–45 all*; Sally Shoemaker: *174B, 183BR*; Mike Shoup: *183BL*; Sonoran Desert Design: *26BC, 38 all, 62*; Steven Sternke, Magic Gardens: *59TR*; Christy Ten Eyck: *49, 80L*; Jeffrey Trent: *69T, 82BL, 89BR, 159TR*; Greg Trutza: *20, 33L, 51, 52–53, 71, 88, 90B, 94T, 95T, 149TL, 161TL, 171T, 179L, 181BL*; Carol Valentine: *150–151T*; Armijo and Terra Vessel: *79B*; Paul Weiner: *95B*; Margaret West: *72–73 all, 162T, 172*; Nick Williams and Asosciates: *93T*; Zischke Studios: *66–67*

acknowledgments

The editors want to thank the following for their contributions to *Gardening in the Southwest*.

FOR INFORMATION ABOUT CLIMATE: **Gregg Garfin**, Institute for the Study of Planet Earth, University of Arizona, Tucson; **Dave Gutzler**, Department of Earth and Planetary Sciences, University of New Mexico, Albuquerque; **Charlie Liles**, National Weather Service, Albuquerque; **Nathan Mantua**, Climate Impacts Group, University of Washington, Seattle; **George Taylor**, Oregon Climate Service, Oregon State University, Corvallis.

FOR INFORMATION ABOUT HORTICULTURE AND DESIGN: **John Begeman**, Pima County Cooperative Extension, Tucson; **Paul Bosland**, Agronomy and Horticulture, New Mexico State University, Las Cruces; **Dave Ferguson**, Horticulture, Rio Grande Botanic Garden, Albuquerque; **Ron Gass**, Mountain States Wholesale Nursery, Glendale, Arizona; **Gail Haggard**, Plants of the Southwest, Santa Fe; **Glenn Huntington**, Living Desert Zoo and Gardens, Palm Desert, California; **Denise McConnell**, Springs Preserve, Las Vegas; **Bob Morris**, Clark County Cooperative Extension, Las Vegas; **Gary Paul Nabhan**, Center for Sustainable Environments, Northern Arizona University, Flagstaff; **Judith Phillips**, Bernardo Beach Native Plants, Albuquerque; **Janet Rademacher**, Mountain States Nursery, Litchfield Park, Arizona; **David Salman**, High Country Gardens/Santa Fe Greenhouses, Santa Fe; **Dennis Swartzell**, Mountain States Nursery, Las Vegas; **Jackie Wilson**, Amarillo Botanical Gardens, Amarillo.

index

Pages in *italics* include photographs.